My Men, Mick, and Me

Andee Baker

DEDICATION

To all the people in my life who made me laugh,

and to those who encouraged my writing.

Contents

My Men, Mick, and Me

Prologue

"Just My Imagination":
Me and Mick in New York

Here in New York City, arguably, the entertainment capital of the world, I wait to catch a glimpse of Mick Jagger, herded across the street from the Beacon Theatre onto the sidewalk with perhaps 60 or 70 other fans, on fall day November 1, 2006... I say hi to L'Wren, as she enters through the backstage door, shouting until she acknowledges me with a wave. No one else seems to know of her long-time relationship with Mick.

Yes! Now Mick has emerged from his chauffeur-driven vehicle and makes his way to the edge of the sidewalk to give us fans a few minutes of his time. He waves and seems to smile at me. Hey, let me try to get to the front row to catch a better look. I move to the side, the left side, of the small crowd. He seems to search with his eyes, finds me there, and gives me a direct, questioning look, like, "What are you doing? I lost you there for a second." Wow, I grin, ecstatic. Well, wait, why shouldn't he know me after I attended a bunch of shows up close, wearing my Rolling Stones cowboy hat? Still, to visibly show his recognition of me, hey. Other fans have told me about these moments, and now, they are happening to me. Oh, yeah, oh, yeah.

The title of each chapter, usually about a man or men in my life includes the name of a song written by Rolling Stones Mick Jagger and Keith Richards.

Chapter 1
"Before They Make Me Run":
Reading, Writing, and Boys

Though listed as a Jagger/Richards composition, as are nearly all their songs, "Before They Make Me Run," was written by Keith Richards, who wrote the tune after his 1977 drug bust in Toronto and he sung it in concert and on recordings. Keith epitomized the rock n' roll life style, the ultimate drug addict and carousing cut-up before he settled down in Connecticut with Patti Richards in the 1980's. The lyrics of "Before They Make Me Run," which are all about people dancing and singing, fit my early interests, growing up as a teen in the heyday of rock n' roll. I always enjoyed moving to music and copying the intonations of a lead singer. Grooving to the beat of early rock music and the lyrics, riffs and soul of the Blues, I very much appreciated those genres. So when The Rolling Stones came along, I was ready, ready to rock to a different kind of music, grittier than the Beatles — and become the fan of these musicians who were living their lyrics. Keith tells us he wants to walk before they make him run, and just have some fun, without getting into too much trouble, unlike a few friends of his who didn't make it out alive. For me, Keith and Mick represent my defiant spirit, my inner wild child, as well as the bad boys who attracted me.

I liked school because I was left alone there, except for a pat on the head or a "Good job," once in a while. I remember I had the task of erasing the boards for one grade; an honor, I thought. I hit a few blips, the first in nursery school, what they called state-supported day care back then. The gray-haired teacher in charge, Miss Massey, more than once dragged me by my hair to take me somewhere she wanted me to go, to isolate me from the other kids. After I told my parents—even I knew this bore reporting—they took me out of there. While in nursery school, I never wanted to take naps, but kept myself stiff as a board, so as not to get caught and admonished for not sleeping. In kindergarten and first grade, I remember watching kids cry to escape from getting their shots or eating their asparagus. I was too proud. I think that's when I started studying group behavior, as a budding sociologist.

The next blip came in third grade when Miss Tate caught me talking in class. I had a friend in the row over to the left, one seat ahead of mine. I guess I was commenting on what was going on, but she thought for sure I was talking about her. I didn't stop when she paused. She took me to the far back corner of the classroom and brought out the dunce cap, a large white Pinocchio-like chapeau. This was meant for the "dumb" kids, not me, wasn't it? No, apparently, I had shifted my sharp, acutely aware, always on top of the assignment's role for the clueless student who has to wear the stigmatizing hat. My classmates approached me at recess to ask what the heck had happened? A traumatic occasion, I used it in a workshop when the family therapist John Bradshaw instructed us to go back to our younger selves to talk to them about what they could do differently, how not to cave into our worst feelings. "Everything will be fine," I consoled my mini-me, in school, anyway. And by the way, I thought later, "Try not to irritate the authority figure."

Speaking of authority figures, those two people who spawned me had immense say over what I said and did, as parents usually do. Bradshaw points out that if a three-year-old child is three feet tall, a parent may measure at twice the child's height. The parents would loom over their offspring like an extinct wooly mammoth or relatively, like the larger steppe mammoth would look to an average adult. Both of mine had prodigious intellectual and verbal gifts, but came from poor Eastern European immigrants, scratching out a living for their family. Graduating second in her high school class, Mom went to business school, Dad going to college on the GI Bill after I came along.

I was so much more like my dad Jack than my mom Betty: he and I understood each other, both artsy, unconventional, neither very good in math. My mom had auburn hair highlighted in the beauty parlor by red hair dye, high cheekbones and beautiful skin. She would tell me, "You look like your father." He and I shared dark brown hair and strong features, but her remark unsettled me, as I observed his prominent moustache, atypical for the times, whether bushier or trimmer over the decades. He took me everywhere with him, replacing the imaginary male child he wished he had, fostering the comfort I would grow up to feel with boys and men from spending so many hours in his company. We snacked at soda fountains or in the Rathskeller at the university, talking, or most commonly, me listening to him pontificate about politics and personalities, whether famous figures or just friends and relatives. A black and white photo likely taken by my mom when I was about four, showed us facing each other in profile, me standing on a high concrete step to reach his height. His large aviator sunglasses from the Air Force that he put on me for the photo covered most of my face, except for my outsized smile, mirroring his, our eyes crinkled up with happiness.

Boys I liked early on, not including the two I stood between in the photo from kindergarten kept by my dad in his wallet, were Jesse and Mark. Jesse had large, heavy-lidded blue eyes, and once when he caught me staring in class, he favored me with a slow wink. My neighbor across the street, Mark, an intelligent, freckled red-head and I would spend hours talking, trading comic books and baseball cards, and watching his train set traverse the elaborate tracks his dad had built in the basement. He and I made sure we were square dance partners in 4th and 5th grade, the second year surreptitiously trading spots with other kids in line to wind up across from each other to ensure our partnership. About the same height, no one challenged our ruse, as our classmates stood around us in our two lines, watching our maneuvering.

Mark's dad one day interrupted our friendship by announcing to his son that the time had come for him to have a male best friend, dropping me, the girl across the alley. I told my parents, teary-eyed at my loss. They considered talking to Mark's dad but dropped the idea, noting that in those days, Mark's father probably didn't even believe in women working, like my mom did. Looking back, I recall them hinting in low tones that Mark's dad worried that his son might turn gay if left to bond with a female during his formative years. As we all turned a little bit older, my friend Deedee developed a crush on Mark and would chase him, running after him when we played outdoor games, embarrassing me.

The next boy I remember liking came from the neighborhood too, a number of blocks away. I encountered him in the last place I lived in the big city before my family moved out to the farthest, wealthiest suburb. On a summer day following sixth grade, prepubescent, I went for a walk and met a cute boy with dark, almost black hair, with matching long, thick eyelashes that shaded his blue eyes. For some reason, Jamie and I began to roll down the steep grassy hill together in his large back yard. About the same height, hugged together. we rolled down the hill, slowly and then faster, in the soft grass, touching front to front, our arms around each other. We exchanged very few words but found enough of them to plan to meet again, to practice the same maneuver next day. You know what? Out of all the fun I've had, this hug/roll was about the best thing that had ever happened to me and continued as a highpoint in my memory, yes, until this very moment. Wow, the male/female energy, the innocence and yet barely submerged carnality of this full-body hug. We knew it was forbidden, but did we care? No. I did pick up a grass stain or two, and a bunch of loose grass after his dad had mowed. I smiled all the way home and for some time afterwards.

The neighbors had likely witnessed – and probably gossiped about — these two kids, soon to be teens, pressed together and for some reason, rolling, rolling, rolling to the bottom, and then beginning the process again. After the better part of a week, his mother came out and put a swift halt to our activity at the end of one of our rolls. I tried to hang my head to show remorse when my parents confronted me, hearing about us through his parents. In a harsh tone, my mom asked, "What were you two doing?" but I couldn't completely hide my joy in the pleasure I felt privileged to experience.

I loved my male teachers, in late grade school and junior high, first Mr. Trock, who single-handedly pulled Joey T out of his chair to place him on top of the wooden

Xmas tree nailed to the gymnasium wall of our classroom. His legs dangling while the class laughed, Joey never fidgeted again, his undiagnosed, then-unheard-of ADD cured forever, at least in public. Today Joey would likely go to the principal's office, a problem child, and maybe have to take his Ritalin or Adderall. The man instructing us in seventh grade, Mr. Ratnor, had us doing complex semester-long projects, centered on a country of our choice. I picked Brazil, and sent away for information, surprising my parents when posters and packets arrived from far-away travel bureaus, addressed to me. For many years, I kept my completed work, compiled in a folder with a cover decoration of a cut-out coffee cup and saucer with paper steam curling up from it. In eighth grade, Mr. Tosco led us in Army songs, later letting us "put on a show," with musical direction by my pal Sammy down the road, who could play just about any show tune on the piano. My parents were none too pleased when I came home singing, "My gal's a corker, she's a New Yorker…she's got a pair of hips, just like two battle ships." Finally, in ninth grade, my English teacher Mr. Haas hired me first to babysit, and then to record student grades, paying me to assist his teaching. He also challenged me intellectually, telling me that I could go further with my own ideas in my papers.

Never confident in my own appearance, my ninth grade algebra teacher didn't help when he made fun of my then much curlier, short hair, wet from showering after gym class in the previous period. I stood at the board, on his orders, while he put me down in front of the whole class, for my hair and my performance, none too competent, in my worst subject. My classmates didn't laugh, possibly feeling sorry for me, but a couple of them later told me I blushed up there. His treatment ended my positive run with male instructors. During high school, someone told me I looked like Mick Jagger, and I smiled, not knowing whether to take it as an insult or a compliment. I remember asking if he thought I looked like a man, and he said no, just a facial resemblance. I think it's the lipsI Someone at an art gallery told me that recently too, when I spoke of my writing on the Stones, which was almost as much of a shock as the earlier comparison. I grinned and said, "Really?"

I wore skirts to attend class all throughout high school, but as soon as blue jeans came into fashion, that was it for me, my almost-always chosen garment for my lower half. Rarely wearing dresses, I gave up heels a few years after I tried them on. At one point during the height of the counterculture, I joined the throngs of both males and females wearing the uniform of flannel shirts and jeans. At the time, I wore almost no make-up, giving up elements of traditional feminine appearance; my male counterparts had grown out their hair and picked up a strand or two of "love beads," along with leather bracelets, and bandanas. One characteristic of Mick Jagger I admired was his androgyny in style and mannerisms, coming into play early on with scarves and studded belts, most obviously during the late 60s into the 70s. Ossie Carter designed Mick's jump-suits, sometimes cut to his waist, made of silky material, with lacings and sequins, in light, bright colors not typically worn by men, even lead singers. His collar-length hair, jewelry, and make-up, including eyeliner and lipstick prefigured the punk bands looks of the 80s.

When I entered the U down the street, the big regional campus of the University of Wisconsin in Milwaukee, I wasn't expecting to meet the Polish kids from the South Side. I had come from the North, the Northeast to be exact, and before that, the West Side, in grade school. I had thought most people were German and Lutheran, most people in the US that is, for the longest time, with a few Catholics, here and there, and a few Jews. I came into college with no idea how hard the work was, no concept that I might have to study for decent grades.

In the "college boy" realm, or maybe "young man world," I should say, I ran into Brent while paying for my cafeteria food, one of the handsomest creatures I had seen in my relatively short life. He was tall, thin, and blond, with eyes of cerulean and fine, almost delicately formed features. Soon we were talking, and he asked if I wanted to go to the beach with him, at night. What?

Hesitating only a split second, I agreed: "Okay, sure." It was late spring and warming into summer. As we lay on a towel on the sand, after making out for a while fully clothed, he started putting his moves on me. Feeling willing, I quietly announced, "I'm a virgin." After a few denials on his part, "Hey, that couldn't be," and "You're kidding, right?" he finally believed me, straightened his clothing, and sat up, ready to leave. Seeing him later on campus, he wanted virtually nothing to do with me.

Back on the home front, I had meanwhile gone out drinking with a high school friend, at least once a week, often twice, Wednesdays and Fridays, to a "teen bar" some thirty miles away. The bands played cover songs, mostly "fast" ones, such as "Money, (That's What I Want,") covered by The Beatles. Once in a while I'd meet up with a guy called Sunshine who would take me home when my friend went off with other men. He was a sweetheart, but his idea of kissing was more like biting. Even with an occasional "Owww" between lip locks and much pulling away, I couldn't teach him new habits. I wondered if he had learned to kiss from an older neighbor girl, herself perhaps an S and M practitioner.

Too dumb to know not to park in front of the house, I let a couple of guys drop me off there, after a spell of "necking." Once in a while, my parents would lock me out, and then, none too pleased, open the door when I knocked repeatedly. My mom couldn't understand why our mail began to contain scented letters from a sailor furloughed at the naval base nearby. She told me during that period, "You're smart, but you're not mature." I didn't argue back, knowing somehow that her definition of maturity differed from mine, leaving no room for her daughter's casual male/female relationships. One day she typed me a note and slipped it under the door. It said, "Get a job," with a sample newspaper ad attached, relating to something I could possibly do. Not too long after that, she gave me notice that I needed to move out.

The generation gap writ large, I decided later on. This gap, like the Grand Canyon, so long, 277 miles, and so wide, 18 miles in spots, it was almost beyond imagination. Picture the chasm between where people smoked marijuana and took LSD, men had long hair, young women had more sex and different kinds of sex with a number of people outside of marriage, (see the Rolling Stones lyrics "Let's Spend the Night Together," censored by Ed Sullivan), unmarried people cohabitated in pairs and lived together in groups, and the younger generation began to dress casually for all occasions. The older people did drugs too, namely cocktails, beer, cigarettes, caffeine, and a host of pills prescribed mainly to women for maladies ranging from anxiety to depression. Very few divorced, at least among the middle classes, and no one spoke of sexual experimentation, not even oral sex. Most men went directly to work after high school or college, while most women married young and stayed home, at least until their children, numbering an average of three, passed through early grade school.

Did belonging to the older side of the gap include throwing your child out like a piece of used clothing, deemed too damaged, too worn for the Salvation Army? No, probably not, not for most of the graying, martini-drinking crowd over there, gathered at the edge of their side, staring into the giant fissure, bewildered. Abandoning your child, still just in her late teens, was unknown among my friends' parents. But here we were. My mom excused her actions with the statement that I was a "bad influence" on her other kids, my younger sister and brother. That hurt like hell, still does.

The day I left I recall a shadowy figure looking suspiciously like my dad cowering behind my mom, trying to hide. That was not easy to do with his eight inch height advantage, weighing at least forty pounds more. Recognizing him, surprised, I thought how he previously, up to this point, had taken on my side in most matters. We had not talked much of late, him not accepting my choices in becoming an adult, changing from child to woman. He stood there, wordless. "Dad," I called out, letting him know I saw him there. He said, "Sorry, it's your mother's call. I had nothing to do with it," as my mom moved sideways to reveal him, knowing she had his consent. Okay. Another chapter closed, as I mentally waved goodbye to my Daddy's girl self. Where would I go, I had wondered? Shortly before my exit from my home, I found my own classified ad from a young woman looking for a roommate in the hippie-ish part of town. Suitcase in hand, I walked out of the front door of my family home, into the darkness, feeling unmoored, heading to my new abode.

We were on the first floor of an older apartment building with an efficiency-like space, bedroom off the living room, no door, with the kitchen next to the living room. The front door opened directly into the living room. My roommate and I hardly ever saw each other. Her working hours didn't overlap with my work or my class hours. I still went to class even though my heart had long left those school buildings. I remember working for TV Guide, part-time, watching over the teletype machine, pulling relevant postings off as it moved along, clack-clack-clacking away. I wasn't driving then, so caught busses where I could. My building-mates were a rowdy band of what I called for years the affluent delinquents: not in school, working at odd jobs and for almost all of the residents, the men, smoking pot out of a many-armed hookah and avoiding the draft.

Smoking from the hookah, pipes of various kinds, or from joints rolled with cigarette papers or emptied-out cigarettes went nicely with the cigarette habit of many. Almost half of the adult American population indulged in inhaling tobacco regularly in the 1960s. Smoke-filled rooms and hallways were common, populated by coughing people. No one commented on either the air quality or the hacking. If other drugs infiltrated our apartment complex, I didn't notice them. They weren't offered to me. There might have been acid trips taking place around me, perhaps accounting for the walls of one apartment turning completely black one day, literally mimicking the title of the Rolling Stones song, "Paint it, Black."

When I was in the youth-filled apartment building, I became involved in a heist of t-shirts from our teen bar thirty miles away. Young people between eighteen and twenty-one could drink there legally, unlike in the city. Not wanting to steal the shirts, a member of the group, hearing my attitude, assigned me the role of look-out, which I performed reluctantly, leaving my post early. About a week later, my roommate and I answered the door, after gathering that police officers had entered the building. We denied involvement in the crime, the realization that the guys had pinned it all on us dawning slowing. After a few shakes of my head, and "I know nothing about it," one cop finally said to me, "You have brown eyes. Brown-eyed people are honest," and with that, he let us close the door. I felt relief sweep over me, like I had drawn the "Get Out of Jail" card in Monopoly.

The residents found out I was a virgin, a status they deemed unacceptable for a renter in their building. They fixed me up with a classical guitarist, which made for a typical losing-your-virginity story, a painful rite of passage, over fairly quickly. His kindness helped the situation, including when he decided we should try the sex thing again. After that I mostly just shared a bed with this guy named Glenn, cuddling up through the fall into winter chilly nights, no sex, just body contact, with all underwear on. After several weeks away from home, I lost my key, and discovered someone had used it to take things out of my apartment, what a surprise. When I told my mom my stuff had been stolen, she told me to come back, no more questions asked.

Before I went back home, I had a whirlwind sex session of thirty-six hours with Jared, a man I met up at the University Wisconsin, Madison, at a dance. I knew he was out of my league looks-wise, a tall mesomorph, blond, with chiseled features. Dancing a waltz in his arms, I felt a nervous attraction. When he called me to ask if he could come down to Milwaukee, I guessed what he had in mind. I didn't turn him down, using a friend's vacated apartment for our tryst. He tried every position in every room, showers in between, a short respite and he wanted another go at it. The guy was at his peak of powers, I'm thinking, and would not stop. At this point, I was inexperienced in the art of lovemaking, yet I did feel more excitement physically than I had up to this weekend. It was very close to the "zipless fuck" of Jong's *Fear of Flying*, not much conversation, and no promise of more later on. Jared called me again for a repeat engagement, but I said I was busy.

Not too long after that, I started working full-time in the office of a plumbing company, and soon, I met Charlie.

We had both failed out of our school programs, me in undergrad liberal arts, and him in grad school in math. My admissions office contacted me in my sophomore year to ask if perhaps I wanted to drop out, as I was not working up to my potential. I insisted I would try harder to live up to the potential of my SAT scores and high school grades. A chance I had to do better came when enrolled in the psych statistics class required for my major. The good-looking, red-bearded TA, perhaps six years my senior ran into me in a restaurant near campus and kindly offered to help me, to tutor me for free. I told him no, that nothing could rescue me now, as I didn't have the will to succeed. I've never forgotten his kindness.

Interlude: "Get Off of My Cloud": Stones, Early Days:

When prompted by their new manager Andrew Loog Oldham, who had done PR for the Beatles, Mick Jagger and Keith Richards started writing their own songs. All of sudden, the boys in the band began hitting it big. After giving "As Tears Go By" to Marianne Faithful, Keith Richards came up with the riff for "Satisfaction," caught on tape before he fell asleep. "Get Off of My Cloud" became their second hit, figuring in my first nights in that youth-filled apartment building. One day I heard strange sounds coming from above the bedroom-area ceiling. Listening more closely, I made out the words sung-shouted by Mick Jagger: "Hey you! Get offa my cloud. Two's a crowd on my cloud." Hmmmm. I pondered that for years.

Chapter 2
"2000 Light Years from Home":
Charlie, the Prince on the White Horse

Since I didn't go away to college, I had only lived in one other place besides "at home" before I met Charlie. My family moved several times in my childhood, the last between my freshman and sophomore year in high school, a difficult transition that forced me to make all new friends and adjust to different academic standards. When I met Charlie, I moved into a tiny place, which felt like my own heaven, however small, because it was my first time "2000 Light Years" away from my parents' control. Charlie and I stayed mainly at his apartment until he joined the US Navy and went off to basic training out east. He came home, and we married, embarking on our new life in another state, Ohio, a territory completely unknown to either of us.

While the song "2000 Light Years" likely refers to getting "away" by tripping on acid or other psychedelics, Charlie and I were off on own journey away, into similarly uncharted lands, moving by ourselves, with no friends or relatives nearby. So much more at ease in my new life, I didn't visit my parents or hometown for four years. I had no urge to return.

I threatened to leave my husband Charlie after a few years, but not out loud. He'd say, "You'll never leave because you wouldn't know what to do," meaning I couldn't make my own way without him. Maybe he thought I would curl up in a ball, huddle in a corner until I withered away, or he hoped I would, anyway. I was the one who was planning my escape. Should I run away in the middle of the night or should I run away with another man or should I just tell him, bye, bye, it's over now?

Before I met Charlie back in the late 1960s, I was hanging out at O'Grady's on Milwaukee's Farwell Street where the band "The Shags" played. A favorite spot for college kids and other post-high school grads still finding themselves before settling down, the smoke-filled club had very dim lighting, posters of bands on the walls, and when the music started, a psychedelic aura. One night, a couple of guys approached me, introducing themselves as Brent and Brian. These slightly older grad students didn't seem exactly my type, but they told me they had just the man for me. Their pal Charlie and I and the boys met for dinner. They all drank quite a bit, Charlie more than anyone, and from then on, we weren't apart much. I worried that he had a drinking problem, but no, that was just ale by association, increased consumption when going out with his buddies.

They were right about the two of us. We made a good match, at the time, anyway. We both had intellectual dads, though his had the credentials mine lacked. Both of us were the oldest, he with a younger sister, and me with the two much younger sibs, a miscarriage goofing up the careful spacing between the first and second. Both of us were and are the take charge types, him more than me, both fire signs, his even stronger than mine, Aries the Ram over Sagittarius, the Centaur. He wanted "a companion." Yeah, me too.

When Charlie's parents first met, his mom Cora had started her master's in Physics and his dad Duncan worked on his doctorate in chemistry. She had gone to Barnard College, the "sister" school of his university, Columbia. One guess which one dropped out to marry and start a family, going on to run the PTO and the Music Parents group. If two people could be more dominant, more domineering than my parents, here they were. Charlie drove us across the eastern half of the US to meet them. We were all supposed to go hiking early in the morning and swimming in the ocean, but Cora didn't have to go. She was busy cooking and cleaning. She found enough time to take me shopping for the bathing suit I didn't bring, my first excuse for not wanting to take the plunge into the Atlantic. It was pink on the top and had a cranberry-colored skirt, two toned, with thin spaghetti straps, as I recall. I didn't want it, but she insisted.

Worse was yet to come out on the ocean, after launching off in Padanaram, on Buzzard's Bay, near

South Dartmouth, Massachusetts, when Duncan told me it was time to "Jump in." "I can't swim," I told him. No matter. Apparently, this was a rite of family passage, or else one created just for me, the girl.

Okay, here goes: splash, into the cool but not freezing brine. Hand-crafted by Duncan and Charlie's grandfather, the wooden sailboat began to drift further and further away, not surprisingly, given my feeble attempts to move closer. I floated on my back atop the salt, hoping that Charlie would rescue me from the brine, as he had appeared to save me from permanent singlehood. It took him a while to traverse the distance. A thought started to pass through my mind, and stopped. "What if I died out here?" I pushed it away, having prepared for it earlier, in anticipation of the boat trip and my inauspicious entry into the ocean. It was very peaceful here, no noise whatsoever, except for the rhythmic movement of the waves. Hearing something hit the water, I thought I saw in the distance, the speck of Charlie diving from the boat, presumably coming to get me. Yes, here, he comes, arm over arm. Could he make it? Ah, yes, soon I was okay, safely towed back under Charlie's arm, if a bit shaken. When we reached the boat and he pulled me up into it, his father Duncan just made a hoarse noise in his throat resembling the first half of a chuckle, not saying anything. Yeah, other than the idea that he might have let me drown, what was there to say, anyway?

After that, I remember a dinner, not unlike *Annie Hall*'s scene of the family meal with the guest Alvy Singer, Diane Keaton's boyfriend played by Woody Allen. We all sat around a long mahogany Victorian table, with silverware and glasses, accessories I helped place alongside the dinner plates with flowered borders. "Do you eat pork?" "Do you have to eat kosher food?" Cora and Duncan asked about my eating habits. The parents treated me as if I was a specimen from the Portuguese community living in a different part of New Bedford from their family home in the city. "We know this one Jewish couple from Woods Hole," Cora said, drawing on whatever customs they had gleaned from them. "No, no food restrictions," I explained, noting those went with more Orthodox or at least Conservative branches, rather than the secular, cultural kind of my immediate kin. I knew Charlie was clearly atheistic and later found out that Duncan advised him never to tell anyone he had raised his son not to believe in God, or gods of any kind.

After my visit, unprecedented by other young women Charlie might have chosen to bring home but didn't, his parents wrote the following words to him, recalled here:

"Dear Charles. We enjoyed meeting Andrea but really advise against you two getting married. We don't think she is the right woman for you.

23

You need someone with a college degree. We hope to see you again soon.

All our love,

Mother and Father."

I was devastated. Yes, there was the swimming incident and also the awkward questions at dinner about my religious practices. Unrecognized by Duncan, Charlie's family had much in common with my family of origin, largely non-practicing, non-religious Jewish people, not that far from Duncan's religion of militant atheism, privately if not publicly held. He had told Charlie not to declare his anti-theistic heritage on any documents, so Charlie put down "Christian" on his Navy enlistment forms. That was before the label took on the fundamentalist, evangelical meaning among some folks. I told him to pick a more specific religion to sound more genuine. I always said Charlie and I had a "mixed marriage," me the agnostic and him the atheist. I converted to atheism, in front of him, anyway. Putting away the letter, Charlie assured me that if his parents wanted to keep their relationship with him, they would have to accept me.

On balmy nights on the east side of town, Charlie and I walked in darkness, holding hands, pretending we were Maria and Tony from *West Side Story*. We sang

"Tonight," "One, Hand, One Heart, and "Somewhere" our favorite, with its lyrics describing a place and time where we could be together freely. We were serious about each other. These songs were hard to top in our alienated, bound-together youth in the thick of the counterculture, on one side of the very real generation gap. He let me tackle "I Feel Pretty" on my own, not even attempting the "Jet Song" sung by the macho, cigarette-smoking, finger-snapping gang members in the film. Neither of us was the type to learn "Cool," though we looked up to that ethos from afar, not seriously aspiring to embody it. We were anything but cool. That Lenny Bernstein sure knew how to write music, and, combined with a young Sondheim's lyrics, the pieces were marvelously evocative for young lovers everywhere. At the time we didn't dwell on the tragic ending of the film somewhat following the plot of Shakespeare's *Romeo and Juliet*. We also sang "You'll Never Walk Alone," and "Climb Every Mountain," probably doing a better job with these spiritual show tunes, having practiced those more in grade school choruses.

Though he came from a classical tradition of listening and violin lessons, and I stood (or danced) more firmly in the rock and blues world, we overlapped with our exposure to musicals, very popular with our parents in common with most adults during those times.

As we sang without much concern if anyone heard us, I knew only certain types of young people would do that, me, feeling mushy and inclined to perform and him, a nerdy math guy with a pocket protector, falling in love. Interactions like that led to marriage, a scant six months after we met; foolhardy, looking back, yet extremely satisfying in the moment. The decision, mainly on his part, seemed like the right thing to do. I was living in a tiny apartment, just a place to sleep, waiting for him to finish his basic training in the Navy. I was like a first mate to his captain's status in the family. I had no post high-school degrees, not much life experience and few possessions. I was 21.

"It was the best of times, it was the worst of times," as Dickens wrote. Or as Charlie used to say about his life when in the mood, chanting: "To-morrow, and to-morrow, and to-morrow, creeps in this petty pace from day to day," from *Macbeth*, I later learned. Hmm, I did not know that Macbeth had expressed his indifference to his wife's death in these lines, very stoic, like Charlie, or as Charlie would have others see him. He knew longer quotes than I did, and more of them. I'm not sure if he learned them from his dad or picked them up at the big U in Madison, Wisconsin. As an atheist, he also loved the ending of the "tomorrow" passage, "It is a tale told by an idiot, full of sound and fury, signifying nothing," borrowed later on by William Faulkner. Once we stared into a toilet bowl, the water swirling around and down, agreeing that life had no purpose or meaning.

Unlike Charlie's parents, mine were thrilled for Charlie and me. My dad Jack did say, seeing my new Anglo last name, "Baker, mmm…Did you make that up?" Betty had suspected no one would want me, considering my weight, quite high in my late high school into college years. She commented that the Navy guy I met at the teen bar who sent me letters steeped in cologne probably mistook my intelligence for emotional maturity. Way to support your daughter, Mom! Immediately after our very small wedding led by a Justice of the Peace, attended by my parents and my best friend, my mom held a very small reception for the five of us, a dinner out at a restaurant in town. I wore one of my mom's knit suits for the festivities, cream-colored, with grass-green trim. She arranged for a hotel room with her boss's hotel, the Red Roof Inn. After that one-night "honeymoon," we left for Cleveland and Charlie's new job with the US Navy Finance Center.

We had a good time for a while. I ironed his Naval uniforms, and learned to cook a few dishes. I made pork chops with onion soup gravy and a dish called "Poppin' Fresh Barbecups." That one had won a Pillsbury baking contest for a California man in 1968, using muffin tins lined with pressed biscuit dough for crusts, filled with cooked ground beef flavored with barbecue sauce, onions, and a dash of brown sugar, and topped with shredded cheddar cheese, baked for twelve minutes at 400 degrees or until the cheese melted. Charlie expressed pride in me when these entree muffins, these sloppy joe cupcakes, became hits at potluck dinners.

He cooked only outside, with his barbecuing tools. Charlie was good with tools. When he was three his dad took pictures of him with a hammer and a pliers, standing in front of his very own tepee. I always wanted those shots to introduce the topic of "gender roles" while teaching Soc 101. Charlie didn't say much until you got him going, and then he turned into a veritable Arlo Guthrie embarking on the tale of "Alice's Restaurant" with "circles and arrows" on the blackboard he installed in his den to work out formulas and grand systems diagrams. He often wrote on napkins too, during dinner. We took togetherness to a high level back then, like many couples, spending all our free time together. The two of us had moved from our home state at the behest of the military, knowing nary a living soul outside of each other.

I soon went back to school, under Charlie's directive, because he thought that, unlike him, "I liked it." This time it took. I worked various part-time jobs too, the best ones assisting professors in college and grad school. As an older, non-traditional, "adult student" in my early to mid-twenties I met others coming back for another shot. We had fun and studied too, appreciating our second chance to go to college. Trouble was, I met men who turned my head, particularly when Charlie showed clear signs of resisting my increasing pull for independence.

Fortunately for us both, I wasn't driving at all, just taking the bus and getting rides from other people. I was a nicer person then, sticking around until the other person was ready to leave anywhere.

We used to disagree quite a lot, enjoying the oral combat. He had been on his high school debating team, and interacted with his educated and pugnacious mother and father. I had fought with my smart parents too, my father a voracious reader and practiced talker with a large vocabulary, civil and profane. He used it to insult his opponents if logical and factual dissection of their words failed, or sometimes simply if he didn't like the person.

Even if he did, his own insecurities could prompt an outburst. You never knew when Jack's zingers were coming. One of those could knock me out cold and stick in my mind forever. Once, in an elevator with just Betty and me, he turned to me and said in a light tone, "We like your sister better because she sends us cards." My mom said, "Jaaaa-aack." I managed a feeble laugh, thinking he might be joking…stuffing the possibility that he wasn't, and the sadness that went with it.

A couple of talks I remember as major warning signs happened after a few years of marriage, one centering around having and raising children. Before we wed, when I said I wanted one or two kids, he countered with four. Houston, we have a problem. The first major conversation was when Charlie announced it was time for us to have kids. I said, okay, "Who's going to take care of these kids?" Charlie answered, "You are." "One hundred per cent," he said, unless he took them out somewhere like the zoo, on a weekend. This idea, I figured, was simply Charlie following his old man's forceful lead, but, hey, this was the early 1970s, and gender roles were changing. I had thought, anyway. My answer to myself then and to him too, later on was, "I think I'll go to grad school instead." My sociology profs had encouraged that option for me.

When things got really tough with Charlie and me, the verbal arguing escalated into yelling and banging. I thought nothing of slamming doors, a habit my future boyfriend Arthur shouted right out of me. I routinely threw objects, mainly those of softer materials. Kleenex boxes were light and made a big bang sound when they hit the wall. I suppose a corner could have hit Charlie. I wasn't really aiming for him. I got my own behavior back at me, more directly, more seriously, one day when he hit me. I can't remember where his hand landed. Was it a slap in the face or a glancing blow to the head or shoulder? I decided I wasn't going to wait to find out if he would do it again. Did that bodily blow kill the marriage? I think it deadened the piece of my heart that had thought he held my best interests equal to his own. It became a physical punctuation to two verbal exchanges that marked the beginnings of the very real end. The prince's white horse had run off into the woods.

When he was working at the small software company, I'd attempted to have him call me if he'd be late, either at the office or out with his co-workers. He'd explain that he didn't want to embarrass himself by leaving his colleagues to use the phone. I never really accepted that, resigned as I was to him logging extra hours in the evenings and sometimes on weekends. That was the same period I beat him regularly at foosball and in his frustration, he put our game away at the back of the closet. I had practiced while he was at work before his unemployment.

The second major conversation came after Charlie got laid off, not a good time for him, considering his emotional investment in his work. I asked if we could go to California, something we had often discussed when we first married. I had met a husband-wife team teaching out of UC Sacramento who both expressed interest in my work, my research for my doctorate. When the Navy released Charlie before he finished his full term of service through Nixon's de-escalation of Vietnam, we found that employers would fly him out for interviews in Los Angeles, but not to San Francisco. Now he had enough money saved to pursue any option he chose. I will not forget his reaction to my question about changing grad schools and locales. He moved a quarter turn, stood still, facing away from me, not turning around. He didn't say a word. That was the end of that. While more extreme then his usual monosyllabic answers to my questions about our relationship, this standing silence was qualitatively different for me. I knew then that my accepted position of submission up to this point had done me in, and had finished us off as a couple.

Charlie had a hard way to go during the late 60s to early 70s with the rise of the feminist movement. When my turn came to host the consciousness-raising group, since no men were allowed, Charlie had to vacate our apartment. In a way it was the counterpart to "no girls allowed" in the boys' clubhouse, akin to Freud's latency period, where each sex stuck to their own. As in the Black Power movement, women needed their own spaces for a time, while many of us continued to stay in relationships with men. As pointed out by some theorists, women were the only minority group who lived with the oppressor, at least if they were heterosexual. Charlie did not appreciate leaving his home, "his castle."

Knowing my marriage would likely end, I became involved with Sam, a student slightly ahead of me in grad school. I heard Charlie crying in the shower, as my relationship with Sam continued. He wouldn't tell me why. He came home early once and found us sitting very close together, completely stoned. Charlie and I were on a plane, on our way down to a cruise ship, to join his parents, no less, when he asked me directly if I was having an affair, and I told him yes, and he guessed who my paramour was, Sam, who he had met. He demanded I give Sam up and I told him I didn't know if I could. He later told me he wanted revenge and almost went out to buy a gun. "Who were you going to shoot?" I queried. He said he had pondered that question and centered on Sam, blaming him more than me, as the man who took his wife from him.

During the cruise he wandered about on the ship and on shore and spoke of unlikely happenings, mainly in his head. I told his parents a little about the probability of their son going "crazy," or becoming delusional. They said no one in their family had ever had a mental illness. Really? Knowing both of them and their son, I suspected the validity of that notion, thinking "cover-up" or denial. . His mother did tell me on the cruise, five years after we married, that she could tell her son was "attracted" to me. She seemed to reveal this as an apology to me for her earlier advice to him to drop me, and also in sympathy for my caretaking of him in his distressed state on the boat. She had observed a distant, confused look in Charlie's eyes, while not acknowledging that he might have a serious problem.

Unfortunately, by this time, Charlie had clearly begun to lose his mind, to become psychotic, soon to become intermittently divorced from reality as well as physically separated from me at about the time he asked me about Sam. We divided our possessions and moved to separate residences shortly after the cruise with his parents, going through with the planned, pre-paid trip, a gift from them, despite our impending crisis of splitting up. Diagnosed at the time as paranoid schizophrenia, his erratic behavior and faulty thinking were to continue for many years after we split up, dividing our belongings, but not losing our caring about the other.

Separating was a painful process I won't forget. When we went through our stuff in the den, I asked him for the real whale's tooth with scrimshaw, a souvenir of him and our marriage. I returned that soon after, not wanting to deprive him of it. Sitting amidst the books we loved, separating them into "his" and "hers" made both of us teary-eyed. Having accumulated so many volumes in college and grad school, I got custody of all the bookshelves he had built, two of which turned out too tall to cart around forever. Charlie made green wood pedestals with slots for the legs, to allow them to stand securely against the walls. I finally ditched them, removing them from the garage where they had stood empty into a dumpster I had rented when I relocated to the southwest. During the move from our common residence after we decided to split, a male friend who had volunteered to help dropped out within an hour, calling Charlie "too bossy."

The day we officially divorced, getting along well, we almost skipped into the courthouse, meeting with a no-cost mediator from legal aid. Under extreme pressure I had promised Charlie, completely unrealistically, that I would never move more than a few blocks away. We both loved our neighborhood in Cleveland Heights. Later, I moved into Arthur's house, after my funding ran out early on a research job. Then I moved out of town for a full-time teaching job and Charlie decided to go to Dallas where he stayed to learn Spanish and avoid paying state income tax. Last time we talked, recently, he told me he had just whipped up a batch of those "Poppin' Barbecups."

Interlude: "All About You": Charlie and the Goat's Head:

Charlie displayed the only thing he really loved about The Rolling Stones: the poster from the album, Goat's Head Soup. *If you haven't seen it, it's a photo of an actual goat's head, with large curving horns, severed from the body, set atop a boiling pot of liquid. It looks bloody, unsavory in all respects. The goat's eyes are half open, the dark pink soup rising up to the bottom of his nose. Unidentified yellowish objects float around the head. Maybe because his sun sign, the Ram, resembles the goat, Charlie very much related to the image. He pasted it in the hallway right next to the door to his den, our second bedroom, reserved for him to work on his large desk with his homemade computer built from assembled parts bought at Radio Shack. I think he knew I would accept without protest the savage image just because it was from a Stones' work. He put it up without asking me if I liked it.*

Chapter 3
"If You Can't Rock Me":
Enter Sam, the Married Man

The song "If You Can't Rock Me" refers to a broken heart, along with the need for thrills which is what I think I wanted, knowing a breakup of my marriage was inevitable. Charlie and I had lost much of the intimacy between us, so I had formed friendships with other men to engage in conversations with special emphasis on emotional stuff and relationship interactions. In graduate school, I continued to pursue these intimate conversations with my fellow (male) students to discuss sociological ideas. In Sam I found a kindred free spirit, and while our intent did not include sex, we let it happen. In recent years, the Stones organization has printed a tank top for women that says, "If you can't rock me, the Rolling Stones will." I have that shirt, unworn, but valued for its humor and confidence, the forthrightness of the slogan. At the time, I would never have said I was willing to have a man other than my husband "rock me", but I acted it out with Sam.

I had begun to think of leaving my marriage, to consider it. I knew if I went through with anything sexual, especially something that developed into a serious connection, that Charlie and I were done, kaput, over. Our physical intimacy had dried up, so to speak, an issue that concerned him. Our verbal exchanges, once so intellectually alive and heated, had dwindled too, which concerned me. Emotionally we had grown distant, me not bugging him to talk about what was going on and where we were going. After we separated, Charlie told me he took everything he didn't like about me and dumped it all into a "trap door in his head," where it slid down into the tissues of his brain.

At age sixteen, my dad told me about the affair he and the librarian were having: a confession that stayed stuck in a crevice in my psyche. I remember thinking "Oh no, my poor mom," and also wishing he had not told me. I didn't care for the role of his confidante, and I had the feeling his indiscretion would influence my own behavior down the line, and not for the good. Swallowing hard, to alleviate the wad of saliva that had formed as he revealed this information, I couldn't stop the ache in my now wounded solar plexus. When Sam and I initiated our affair, I knew, aside from the "anything goes" atmosphere of the 1970s, that my father's behavior toward my mother had legitimized infidelity for me, against my code of morality and despite my grief for my mom. I brought it up with her many years later, and she said she knew, and that they had problems at the time. My careless attitude toward returning library books from adolescence onward emulated my father's idea of not taking rules of society too seriously. He never paid fines for his late books or mine, telling me not to worry about them. He had modeled the behavior that he, and by extension, his daughter, me, could practice infidelity without serious consequences, or I hoped so, anyway.

Being on my own, while a little scary, was invigorating. I felt I had finally turned from something of a child bride at 21 into an adult of sorts. I supported myself with my part-time earnings, staying for a time alone in our place. I did love living there alone, with both bedrooms mine instead of the den for him, and the fenced patio above the garage. Where Charlie used to barbecue, I now sunbathed, looking pretty good in a bikini after a major weight loss. I felt free, no longer in his terminology, Charlie's "property." After a few months I moved a few blocks away to the third floor attic apartment above a female friend from grad school. Charlie got our old place—he could afford it. Our situation mirrored the past and more recent post-divorce stats, with studies showing that wives' household income and standard of living went down compared to husbands' (see "Gender Differences in the Consequences of Divorce: A Study of Multiple Outcomes" by Thomas Leopold, in *Demography*, 2018, Jun; 55 (3) 769-797.)

When I told Charlie who my partner in the marriage-ending affair was, he said he was going to buy a gun to shoot him. I listened very calmly and spoke as if to an addled child, really hearing the pain in what he said, and adding I hoped he wouldn't. Some months later when Charlie's full-blown psychosis flared up, triggered, in timing anyway, by our break-up, he threatened to go and kill the US President, Gerald Ford. We were in his car, at a stoplight, on the way to somewhere. That threat scared me even more, since I had read of crazy people traveling to our capitol city to do just that. He didn't have a reason, other than the voices that directed many of his moves. The voices also told him to put $300 in my mailbox, a bigger amount of cash than he had ever given me. When he wanted it back, I told him no. He had also carried the TV outside, after spontaneously deciding he watched it too much. He left it in front of his place close to the street, and said that someone on a bike picked it up and cycled off with it. It wasn't very big. He soon missed it, but like the cash, he wouldn't see it again.

This triangle between Charlie, Sam and me, with me at the apex, making the decisions, was the first non-familial "triad", the sociological name for a three person-group, I had known, an echo of my family of origin, with my two parents and me, and later, my two siblings and me. Well, an exception to the imbalanced triads of my family and with the men in my life came when Pammy, Rob and I met during that period of my second time around in college. We were all adult students—the two of them singles, and me married—

who started talking in the campus cafeteria. We formed a pure three-person friendship where any arrangement of the three twosomes is just as strong as the other two pairs. These were two of the smartest people I've ever known, and two of the nicest. We had a great time, even though Rob wanted Pammy to be his girlfriend and she had no interest in that. Turns out Pammy came out as a lesbian around that time. Before that, Charlie used to call Pammy "the little brother he never had," not because of her looks or mannerisms, which were traditionally "feminine," but because of her ability to learn chess quickly and play it with him. He kindly gave her money for her college tuition at one point.

A couple of men I thought about and flirted with before Sam included a darkly handsome, but short, charming guy from grad school who was simultaneously studying for his M.D. and Ph. D., and a floppy-haired giant of a man housed in an impressively sculptured body I met through school. He invited me to a party at his lavish home, taking me on a tour of it, and his large garage, filled with his antique car collection. When only three of us remained at the end of the shindig, a mutual male acquaintance told our host I was married, a piece of information I had purposely failed to reveal. After an awkward few minutes, the guy that sabotaged me left, and the host, shaken, called me a cab. Another man who attracted me, I met at a conference in New Orleans, in the city's steamy, sensual atmosphere. I brushed him off at first, changed my mind, and then couldn't find him again, even though I heard from someone he had searched for me too.

The one who stole my heart, my brain, and my sexuality though was Sam, a married grad student. We began talking in his office, usually empty of the other student assigned there. He was two years or so ahead of me, and about the same age. We both had full-time working spouses. I became his unofficial TA at one point in a course called "Drugs and Society," a new course for the times about legal vs. illegal drugs and their effects, and the laws and mores that had sprung up around them.

Our new colleague in grad school, Brad, really liked Sam. I remember him once following us down a sidewalk, Sam striding ahead, and Brad asking me questions about him. His bottom line was, "the guy is so unpretentious." Well, what other kind of friend would I have, I thought. Brad helped me form clearer ideas of what I like in a person. Poor Brad happened to come from a wealthy family but had no inner self-esteem. Ironically Sam came from a wealthy family too but had developed a pretty strong, secure identity. I had to completely cut myself off from Brad when he snidely put down my progress on my dissertation. I asked him if he could support me in the process, and he said "no." He ended up dating a sweet female student who became a good friend of mine later on, and they both eventually finished their degrees.

Very tall and nearly downright skinny, Sam had relatively muscular forearms and legs. He had the posture of someone used to stooping down to others from perhaps growing much taller than his classmates early on. He had fair skin with lots of black hair on his arms and legs. On this head, he had the thickest, glossiest, smoothest hair I may have ever seen on a man, just starting to develop a very few gray hairs. He wore his hair in the style of the times, below his ears on the sides and down a little past the nape of his neck in back, with a heavy lock swooping down over his forehead.

When I asked him if I could touch his hair and he agreed, I pretty much knew I was done for. I had fallen for him. In those days, people I knew, around my age, seemed to slip easily into these no-going-back circumstances. He was the perfect combination of sex, drugs and rock and roll, with his large record collection, some of the best marijuana around, and a variety of pipes and papers for smoking it. And he had SEX, in his own appeal, and in the form of pornography, films he bought or rented from the local adult bookstore to show on his projector at home.

Sam would have me copy the female in the movies, often filmed in black and white, as best I could. He had determined my oral skills could use improving. On my first ingestion of LSD, his teachings were tested, while he stayed completely straight and sober to function as my "guide" for the trip. He had hooked up a set of speakers to the upstairs bedroom and playing all through the hours was Jimi Hendrix. *Are you experienced?* Jimi sang and I thought, "Not that much." I had never heard Sam make some of the sounds he emitted that day. Afterwards, as I was coming down, we went to a nearby neighborhood restaurant. I was still buzzing. Some of our sexual interactions were about him bringing me to a big "O" which he decided, correctly, that I still hadn't achieved. Through much manual manipulation, I finally did, once in a while. Aside from sex and getting super-high on pot (I once remember seeing only flames in front of a red background, as if in a fire) we liked much of the same music, including Eric Clapton with Cream, Stevie Winwood in Traffic, and of course Mick Jagger and Keith Richards of the Stones.

Sam reminded me of how Mick Jagger would pursue sex: unrelentingly. From his dancing style, I doubt Mick would let a woman go without an orgasm too often, if she could have them. Mick said early on (1966) that all dancing was about sex:

> *"I entice the audience, of course I do. I do it every way I can think of… What I'm doing is a sexual thing. I dance, and all dancing is a replacement for sex.*
>
> *What really upsets people is that I'm a man and not a woman. I don't do anything more than a lot of girl dancers, but they're accepted because it's a man's world.*

What I do is very much the same as a girl's striptease dance."

(http://www.timeisonourside.com/moves.html).

Sam taught me that the lengthy, mostly instrumental tune "Can't You Hear Me Knocking" from the Stones' *Sticky Fingers* album could take us through a round of sex, or if it didn't, he'd just repeat the song, pausing to replace the needle at the start of the cut. Instead of dancing like Mick, he sang along to songs he knew, a habit I found seductive. He would sometimes imitate Mick singing, in a sort of caricatured manner, especially at the start of the next song on *Sticky Fingers*, "You Got to Move," a cover of an old blues song. He'd sing, "Ya gah ta mooove, ya gah ta mooove"…each phrase followed by a strange percussive sound, for emphasis. The album cover, designed by Andy Warhol, famously depicted the belted waist, bulging crotch and the hip and upper thigh area of a man clad in tight black jeans with an actual working zipper. To add to the drama, pulling down on the gold serrated hardware displayed jockey-style white underwear. Getting the direct relation of the album's title to the cover image took a little while to surface from my subconscious.

Sam and I traveled to a sociology conference at the height of our affair. On checking into the hotel in a conservative part of Ohio, the clerk balked at giving us a room. After asking who we were, he said, "But you have different last names…" We looked at him thinking, "And your point is…?" After a long silence, he finally handed over the two keys. We used both large beds, hopping from one to the other in our zeal at being away from home together.

Concocting a fantasy, perhaps to lessen our guilt, Sam and I imagined that Charlie and his wife Eleanor would become attracted and act on that. No. We ran it by them as a possibility, however remote, and they spent an evening together once before rejecting the idea completely. Both on the shy side, oriented toward numbers, and black and white thinking, neither could keep a conversation worth having afloat between them. They were more the maintainers, the earners, and, as our marriages evolved, the major cooks in the family.

Sam progressed through grad school casually, with no career goals, not planning on entering the field of sociology, after attaining his degree. When we both talked to our advisor in his office, Sam told the prof that I was the serious student, not him, so he should advise me, "the girl," not him. After finishing his dissertation on marijuana smokers—hmm, what a topic for him, huh? — sure enough, Sam took over the management of the family laundromat back in West Virginia. His dad had become wealthy in a different business before he died, leaving his mom, his sister and him with no money worries and a whole lot of cash in the bank.

Several years later after we had both graduated and lived not terribly far apart, we met again. He flew a little plane, his, I guess, over to see me near my workplace. The attraction had somewhat disappeared. I always speculated that was because our appearances had changed—he didn't like my red metallic glasses, and I wasn't fond of his shorter haircut—knowing in my heart that the passion hadn't lasted beyond the circumstances of our particular situation in the past.

One day in the coffee house, a friend of a friend, Ben, started talking to me while I was looking at a paper I did in grad school. He asked if he could read it and then complimented me on it. Considering I had studied lesbian feminist organizations, I found his open-mindedness impressive. He said, "You are really doing a service" for this group of women, meaning, as a heterosexual, I had explained part of their life style and politics from an empathetic yet outsider's point of view. From a solidly working-class background, Ben worked as an electrician, making good money from a trade that required him to crawl around in tight, hot spaces, over ceilings and inside walls. Luckily, he had a wiry build, and the flexibility needed for the job.

Ben often wore his fatigue jacket, the real olive-colored one from the army. He slicked his hair back, using a gel to keep it in place, contrary to most men then who combed theirs forward or side-parted it. Very intelligent, Ben had invented an electronic device with computer components that I still don't understand enough about to name or describe in detail. He may have put in for a patent. Aside from his apprenticeship for his craft, he was largely self-educated. He complained of acquaintances often wanting him to do electrical repairs, for free or minimal costs. Unlike me, he went to the library alone as a child. A librarian once threw him out for browsing book titles in the adult section.

I knew our relationship had a pre-stamped expiration date about the time he accused me of being "too silly" when we were playing around in bed. How could that be, I thought? His outlook on life was too serious for me. He also objected to me smoking marijuana before having sex, saying he thought I needed it to consider the act with him. He might have been right about that. His drug use happened every so often when he went on what he called a "drinking binge," consuming alcohol for a few days and then stopping for the next six months or so. The biggest problem for me was his racism. I had to convince him to drop his racist language, particularly when he came to pick me up from the racially diverse community college where I taught part-time.

Looking in the classifieds, I saw a position for an electrician in San Francisco. We had talked about both wanting to leave the Midwest, so when I showed the ad to Ben, he jumped at the chance to apply. He achieved the highest test score of any of the three hundred or so applicants. When he accepted the job offer, he asked if I would like to accompany him. I asked, "But Ben, who would support me?" I noted the scarcity of jobs in the Bay area for academics. That took him aback, since his generosity did not extend to taking care of a single adult woman and we weren't committed to marriage or even cohabitation. He wasn't very free with his money in any case, to put it mildly. So off he went.

I talked to him in person some years later, as he proclaimed his happiness with the job, with his adopted city, and with his dating situation. He said since there were so many gay men in San Francisco, his opportunities with women had greatly expanded. He didn't have a current relationship though. He was still available, like me, after Sam moved back home to West Virginia, until I met Arthur.

Interlude: "Satisfaction": Singing with Sam

By far the most avid Stones fan I had so far encountered among my partners, Sam liked all kinds of music. I hadn't seen him play an instrument other than "air guitar," but his singing ability ranked up there, especially when he mimicked whoever sang on a recording. He would emulate the sounds of the instrumental parts too, sounding out the drum, guitar, bass, and horns. As noted above, he sang to the Stones, and we had great sex to their music, which I hear from fans I've met later on is not uncommon. Sam would choose albums and songs he thought suited to the rhythms of sexuality. In his attention to detail, the way he set up the scenes reminds me of the film 10 when Dudley Moore's George and Bo Derek's Jenny make love to Ravel's fifteen-minute Bolero, after Jenny takes a few tokes of a joint.

Chapter 4
"Live with Me":
Arthur, the Alcoholic Artist

This song describes the chaotic goings-on in the singer's house, with a male roommate, like Arthur had before I moved in, and a bunch of kids living upstairs, before meeting a woman he invites in to play her part as a bedmate, and to provide the missing feminine touch. Arthur offered to share his house with me when I prematurely ended my job six months before anticipated, laid off from a project with the federal government. He had paid for the place near the township where his parents lived, buying it, I suspect, with help from their savings. Arthur put my financial needs together with his desire for a female companion, and our mutual interests in the arts, to invite me into his home to replace his roommate, to join him and the only other feminine presence, his Maine coon cat, Ms. Tan.

Arthur's pal, Rodney, thought Arthur and I might make a good couple, so he invited me to meet up with them at a Patti Smith concert. I had spoken to Rodney a few times at the college bar where the Mr. Stress blues band played every Wednesday and Saturday night. Arthur seemed nice, cordial, if a little gruff. He changed places with Rodney so we could watch the show from adjacent seats. Arthur had longish, fine brown hair with a heavy red cast combed back from his forehead, light blue eyes, a beard that could use trimming, and a "barrel chest," as he called it. He was of Scottish and German background, with light skin and a dotting of small freckles. An appealing quality was his singing voice. An appalling quality was his active alcoholism, a trait I soon discovered. Arthur and I embarked upon a relationship that lasted through almost three years, from the end of a temporary research job I had taken after completing grad school, through the first year of a teaching position. I was ready for an equal partnership with a man, both partners working, both having equal weight in the course of the relationship, and hopefully, both communicating openly, to verbally work through issues as a couple.

A prime draw to becoming involved with Arthur was his offer to help me move to my new apartment, right after we met, followed up by coming over at the designated moving time. I found that impressive. He showed up, in a sleeveless sweatshirt and a blue bandanna around his head, ready to move boxes of books and furniture. He was also maybe the first fellow not to "come on" physically right away, to the point that I wasn't sure he found me attractive enough for him. When I brought this up after a few weeks, he said he "was trying to be a gentleman." Arthur was the only guy

I lived with full-time, other than my ex-husband Charlie, and not counting Bobby, who stayed with me on and off for a number of years later on. I considered Arthur my first serious relationship since my divorce from Charlie. Both Charlie and Arthur formed partnerships committed to monogamy.

Shortly after I met Arthur, I lost my full-time job, headquartered in San Francisco, researching cases of domestic violence. The funding ending six months earlier than expected. The two of us briefly discussed if he felt okay with me moving in with him. He said, definitely, since Rodney, his temporary roommate of a few weeks had planned to vacate Arthur's house soon. The convenience factor in the new arrangement meant that Arthur would no longer have to drive to the other side of the city to see me. I didn't have a car. We had spent most every evening together before the decision.

Looked on as a guru more than a drunk by his friends, Arthur compensated well considering how pickled he often was. He liked to cook for people, often making a tasty stir-fry, though tossing in too many spices in large quantities and too much garlic for my palate. Nonetheless, I ate it enthusiastically, plowing into the mounds of rice with chicken bits and onions. I had to swallow and cough occasionally between forkfuls, exhaling to ingest the whole serving. I was happy not to endure Arthur's critiques of the rare dish I prepared early on. I once served us a recipe from my marital days:

pork chops with an onion soup-based sauce that, after his first bite, Arthur refused to eat.

Arthur had friendships with people who didn't care much for me, the new woman in his life, namely Rodney and Victor. The two men didn't want Arthur spending most of his time with me: they wanted him to themselves. In fairness, I felt the same about them. When Arthur and one of these men and I spent time together, I was the third wheel, a lesser part of the triad. Neither of these two were artists. Though Rodney had introduced Arthur and me, thinking Arthur might like me, his initial positive feelings about me cooled to lukewarm at best after I moved in. Rodney, born to wealthy parents, had no apparent need to work. I figured Rodney's moneyed background led him to toss a perfectly good davenport outside in the alley for the trash collectors, while I found the price of zero dollars for the solidly built seating with down cushions ideally suited my taste and unemployed status. I had the scratchy forest-green upholstery re-covered and kept it for over a decade.

His friend Victor held a social service job in state government, driving to visit Arthur every so often, from two hours away in "Oombumbus," as Arthur called it. During one of Victor's visits, Arthur drove the three of us to my workplace on a summer evening. Once there, emerging with papers I had needed, I witnessed Arthur and Victor outside my campus building, in teary paroxysms of drunken gratitude for each other's company alternating with sorrow for their own life travails—I'm not sure which histrionic display won out that night. Luckily for me, though perhaps cold-hearted, Victor would die early on for reasons unknown. I could sense that he would badmouth me until I disappeared, as he may also have done to Arthur's past girlfriends. While alive, he accused me of having bronchitis, entirely possible, with the amount of tobacco I smoked. Most of us smoked a lot back then, even more when you included our marijuana consumption.

Arthur was sensitive and saw himself as the put-upon artist. He accused me of making fun of his scar when I commented on it, a large slash across his chest from an operation. While I admired his artwork, I drew the line at his black and white framed artwork in the dining room. I asked if he could relocate this gigantic photograph of a nude woman with four limbs sprawled out like a butterfly. He accused me of "being just like everyone else," in my artistic sensibility. He implied I had a Neanderthal mentality toward his art, i.e. I had "no taste." True: I simply couldn't concentrate on the "taste" of our food at meals. At least I didn't echo the New York City gallery visitor who reacted in the guestbook to Arthur's "Medusa" piece by writing, "You got a problem with women, Arthur?" I didn't go that far.

A non-living, sometime accomplice to his art, a full-sized skeleton he borrowed from his school's art department, didn't bother me enough to object to its presence, although when Arthur set it up in my living room, it startled me, to say the least. I woke up and saw this bony apparition of "the skelly," sitting in my armchair, appearing to smoke a cigarette, held between his pointer and second fingers—er, right hand bones. I figured Arthur had posed it there as a joke. The skelly appeared in his art, once in profile behind the transparent side view of an extremely slender woman, both standing against a dark background. He framed the photo in an antique walnut oval, giving it the look of a portrait from the distant past. He gave that one to me.

Although I never really hit it off with most of his artist friends, I envied their ability to trade artworks instead of paying each other. One small photo-collage I wish I had purchased from a friend of Arthur's was called "Mr. Potato Head," a mix of human, cardboard and potato elements, a humorous and creative update of the childhood toy. For a group show in Greenwich Village in New York, Arthur created his own photo collage with portraits of each of five artists laid vertically next to each other, an impressive poster, I thought. Once he gave me a handmade birthday card with a photo of his long-haired feline Ms. Tan pasted on the front, along with cut-out balloons. I loved that card.

I did appreciate Arthur's artistic talent, much as I disliked his drinking and hypersensitivity, and really enjoyed kissing him. We shared a long kiss in public at a bar when feeling especially affectionate, applauded by the patrons at the end of it. On the other hand, not much prone to compliments, his creativity led to ambiguous verbal gestures. He called me "Crabcakes," in a warm but mischievous tone a few times. Unsure how to interpret it, a little slow to comprehend, I discovered he didn't choose the nickname to flatter me. He explained, that rather than referring to the golden-browned seafood, he equated me emotionally with the grumpy Lucy of the *Peanuts* comic strip. In one of Charles Schultz' panels, Charlie becomes Shakespearean in describing a less-than-cheerful mood during a rainstorm: "Even my cold cereal tastes like wormwood." Lucy retorts, "How depressed can you get?" driving Charlie into further negativity. Not exactly how I see myself, then or now. Along the same lines, Arthur once compared me to the Venus of Willendorf. Focusing on the "Venus" at first, I puzzled over the "Willendorf" until I looked up photo of the ancient stone statue. I saw her portly roundness, her large breasts and hugely saggy belly. I was not pleased. Besides, my weight was fairly low at the time.

A Scorpio, Arthur showed a jealous streak in response to men I knew, while his interactions with various women created similar feelings in me. Once Sam (the married man,) newly single, came to town and I met him for lunch, just to talk, over Arthur's objections. Arthur's artist friend, Lisa, a woman with an admitted crush on him, took my place when I declined to pose nude for a murder mystery scene photographed with his musician friends. Arthur had photographed Lisa before, once with her new female lover, both wearing either lingerie or nothing at all. I did a couple of sessions too, in various degrees of undress. For the boudoir shots, I insisted he join me in bed, after he set up the camera for time-lapse photography. Those were strange shots, quite naturalistic, except for slight turns toward the camera.

Arthur asked me to sign release papers on another shoot styled and photographed by Lisa, with me in a bustier and underpants, lying on the floor. Luckily, I said no, because not too long after, he accepted an invitation from the gallery director to mount an art exhibit "Arthur Allen: Image Maker" for over three weeks, in my new place of employment. He and the gallery director/humanities professor had a lot in common: cigarettes, alcohol, and of course, a love of fine art. The prof fancied himself an artist of sorts, and a musician, having studied guitar at Berklee College of Music. His writing was excellent, and he edited an arts magazine for a few years. I called him a Renaissance man. The two immediately clicked so well that the prof ended up staying overnight at Arthur's house up in northern Ohio where both had grown up. I quipped after the visit that the double coughing in the morning of these two heavy smokers must have sounded loud and long, if not in complete harmony.

If I had signed off on the photos, my time in the job would have been even more fraught with trouble than it was. Who knows, someone may have tried to fire me for lewd conduct, unbecoming a professor. I'm almost 100 per cent positive that Arthur would have refused my request not to show the pictures. Remember, the first black Miss America, Vanessa Williams (not to compare my looks to hers) lost her crown for appearing nude in *Penthouse* magazine. And that happened not too long after Arthur and I broke up. Having begun a career in show business, her photos resurfaced from her past, published because she had signed a release years before, as a young model. Recently the pageant invited her back to judge the pageant after issuing an apology to her for removing her title.

Arthur was an only child and had trouble with the idea of sharing his bookcases when I moved in with a ton of books, because the funding for my research job ended earlier than I expected. And he wouldn't go along with my idea to buy a cherry coffee table, even with my own money, thinking it too expensive. Unfairly restricting my purchasing, Arthur's words made me chafe at his control, as if I had a rope tied around my shoulders, like a wild horse separated from the herd. I knew if we ever did marry, I would have to agree to take his name, giving up any professional cred I had established. Once we had discussed what would happen if I got pregnant and then later broke up, and he said, "I would keep the baby." Wow. No other discussion: end of story. I wouldn't go along with that plan, no, not after co-creating a conception, however unintended, and not after giving birth. I can't imagine myself giving up a baby to my partner or anyone else. I had once considered becoming a surrogate and rejected the idea almost immediately, knowing the pain of separation from the child would haunt me permanently.

Arthur could be both very funny and very mean or unfeeling when drinking, which, when I knew him, was steadily from 5 p.m. on, every single day. Only after 5 o'clock, you know, and only beer, so no big deal, right? Once he gave a party, and relatively early in the evening, passed out on the couch sitting up. I sat next to him, not knowing what to say to the friends who lingered, people I had not met until that night. I never again considered throwing my own party.

Arthur worked part-time then, teaching printmaking. He had stayed down at the main campus of my regional place of employment for six straight years, working first toward his BA, and then his MFA, all expenses paid by his parents. Arthur told me his parents decided I was after his money. What money? He had a house, sure. Maybe he was set to inherit some bucks from his dad, who worked for the US postal service, and his mom, a homemaker. His schooling took place during the druggiest, and in his case, drinking-est years known to baby boomers: sheer nirvana for Arthur.

We argued quite a bit, though much of the content of those verbal trysts is fuzzy, existing in a backwater of my brain. I saw that compared to the arguments in my marriage, Arthur seemed to have no internal check to prevent remarks that "hit below the belt." Comments about appearance, say, or characteristics beyond one's control were all fair game. I do acknowledge my role in bringing up disagreements and letting them escalate without resolution. One time during a verbal dispute, while I perceived myself exercising considerable verbal restraint, he admonished me: "Don't look at me like that." He said that sitting down, peering up at me, standing, while I stared back in disbelief that he wasn't commending me for not saying anything. If a look could enrage him, combined with his ever-present beer bottle, our relationship had little chance.

Arthur met all the members of my immediate family: my sister, my father, my mother, and my brother. His alcohol consumption appealed to both my dad and that colleague of mine who ran the gallery. Somehow my sister Elaine ended up in Arthur's car with us, visiting for a day on her way to somewhere else. From the back seat, watching him drink from his beer bottle, holding it with the non-steering hand, she emitted a screeching,"Stoooop," indicating that she felt he drove too fast. I was accustomed to both his speed and his constant drinking in the evenings. I listened to them bicker, witnessing his obvious irritation at my sister's attitude. She even told him to stop the car or put the beer away. I think he called her a prima donna or a diva as well as the B-word, afterwards. She was right about the no drinking and driving, of course. Even so, I had not up to that point seen anyone tell Arthur what to do. I had to talk her down during the trip, telling her she didn't have to ride with him again.

At my brother's first wedding in Chicago, Arthur met a few of my other relatives, including my dad, Jack. They hit it off very well, dropping me off and staying out drinking until late. From among the prints Arthur had packed for the trip to show my family, my dad chose an unframed art piece called "Oh, Dear, the Relatives Are Here." When Arthur unrolled it and read the title, Betty let out a gasp, followed by silence from everyone else. I was holding my breath. My mom, Betty, didn't like it at all and never framed it or put it up. No wonder, since the main subject of the artwork, shown leaning back in his lounge chair with a discontented expression, resembled my Uncle Anthony, my mom's brother, a relative especially despised by Jack. My parents often hotly debated the merits and weaknesses of Uncle Anthony. How could Arthur know his artwork mimicked a scene from our family's life? I wonder whatever happened to the print, not my favorite of Arthur's either. I think my brother has it somewhere. The title reminded me of the play "Oh, Dad, Poor Dad, Momma's Hung You in the Closet and I'm Feelin' So Sad," on Broadway in the early 60's.

My father admired Arthur, for making at least something of a living teaching art part-time and selling a photo or lithograph now and then. Jack also had artistic ability, taking classes at the art school for a while. I remember Jack's so-called doodles in ink, sometimes reaching fully detailed portraits in miniature. Both Jack and Arthur had musical talent: Arthur played the guitar, and both were excellent singers, their resonant baritones always on key. Jack used to sing "You are my sunshine, my only sunshine, you make me happy when skies are blue" to me before bedtime when I was little. I remember asking him if those lyrics really meant "me" that I was his sunshine, and he said "Yes." Arthur plunked away on his guitar, vocalizing "I'm gonna sit right down and write myself a letter, and make believe it came from you," á la Fats Waller. I see now that Arthur eventually became the guy my dad wanted to be: a late-marrying holder of a Master of Art degree, a full-time college lecturer, no-children version of himself.

I can only imagine if Arthur and I had married, he would have hung out with my dad, perhaps more than with me. No dirty looks for heavy drinking from Jack, no sir. I have come to believe that Arthur has since stopped drinking, without any concrete evidence beyond his later academic success, online photos showing him looking very serious, and my own wishful thinking.

They made an interesting pair, my dad and boyfriend. Arthur taller by two, or more likely, three inches, assuming each added about a half an inch to their stated heights. Arthur's solid chest overwhelmed Jack's smaller torso, both ambulating on relatively narrow though well-formed legs. Dad had thinning, dark brown almost black hair, already well mixed with gray compared to Arthur's medium reddish-brown, fine hair. Unlike Dad's already high forehead, slowly growing larger with the years, Arthur's pate showed no visible signs of lost strands, though Arthur imagined a slightly receding hairline. Arthur's Scottish blue eyes often twinkled with mischief, almost equaling in intensity Dad's deep brown piercing expression. No one could out-twinkle Jack, or out-glare him either, although Arthur gave it that cold Aryan try when perturbed, enacting the old, "if looks could kill" adage. I could hardly watch the two of them, tossing down their intoxicating beverages. The thought of them as father and son-in-law was too much to bear.

They also shared at least some penchant for physical abuse, with Arthur's choking or strangling me "only" once, giving literal meaning to the phrase, "I could have strangled her (him.)" Jack regularly beat me with first a yardstick and then a belt during my pre-teen into my teen-age years, supposedly for verbal insubordination. My parents had taken off all the locks of the inside doors, which prevented my escape, not to mention disallowed true privacy for any of us in the household. I tried to elude him in closets and by crawling under the bed, but he always dragged me out and started his hitting, only stopping when he grew tired.

For a wedding present, Arthur gave my brother Joel a staged photograph, featuring Lisa, Arthur's artist friend, and the skelly, in a part I had rejected. In the foreground, Lisa laid spread out on the floor, as if dead, with the skelly superimposed on top of her naked body. Dressed as a maid and a butler, the husband and wife Arthur knew who had formed a band resembling the punk rock group "Blondie" stood high up on their staircase, looking down at the Lisa/skelly figure. The couple looked as if they were screaming, with the wife's hands at the sides of her mouth, expressing horror. Arthur had placed a handgun in close proximity to the prone body. This black and white shot was one of Arthur's best pieces. My brother loved it, and immediately hung it on this dining room wall, where it stayed for some time, along with another work that I had given him, a photo-collage of Arthur's eyes and mouth in several rows. Named "I see what I say," the "eyes" piece won a prize from a major museum, entering its collection. The woman who became Joel's second wife removed the skelly photo soon after entering the scene. I have asked Joel for it, and he's repeatedly refused me. He didn't seem to know where it was, stored or perhaps hidden somewhere in his house.

My brother Joel had come along much after me, nearly eleven years, three years after my sister. My parents wanted a boy. He was only ten when I left home, and I didn't see him much through his high school and college years. Besides his charming manner, his athletic, dimpled good looks, and his musical talents, Joel had an apparent ability to get along with people that my father lacked. I came to realize that Joel stood in for a father figure, or alongside my biological one, as an ideal man, a heroic presence for me, a kind, sweet man. Joel's anger sat buried much more deeply than my father's, whose temper could tear a hole in anyone's self-esteem, alienating strangers, friends and family members. Joel understood that as the oldest, I took the brunt of our dad's verbal and physical abuse, including name-calling and paddling. From Joel, I heard how he refused to accept my dad's insults about him and his future spouse, insisting that he stop. With his first wife, Joel raised two kids, a boy and a girl, who remain the closest beings to the children I never had.

Joel's opinion on my male partners, those that he met or at least knew about, became important to me. His perspective on members of our family of origin made sense, because out of the five of us, he was the most neutral, and the friendliest with us all. That his usually tranquil demeanor came at the cost of his drug dependence on marijuana, and to a lesser extent, alcohol, was lost on me until middle adulthood.

Because of Arthur's artistry and the generosity of his gift, Joel held Arthur in awe. He showed his respect and liking by putting Arthur's artwork up on his walls. The only other male partner of mine he has ever met in person, before or after Arthur, was my ex Charlie, who, after introductions, quickly proceeded to get my fourteen-year old brother drunk, causing Joel to barf soon after the bout of fast-drinking. Seeing a vulnerable young male, Charlie knew what he was doing perfectly well, pouncing on the chance to pick on someone. Once I understood the situation, I tried to curtail it, appealing to both the commander and his victim, to no avail. Charlie relished his role too much, while my brother sought the bonding with the older guy, and the intense drinking experience.

Later, I noted in choosing Arthur for my second really serious relationship, I had fallen for the opposite of my ex-husband - except for the extreme drinking. My ex Charlie had fairly quickly cut back his heavy consumption to a minimal amount. When I asked Arthur about his drinking, he told me I was "never, ever to bring up the subject" of alcohol again. His pal Rodney had thrown out a hint or two of Arthur's drinking problem. I had soon observed an overflowing wastebasket of beer bottles, but it took me a little longer to realize that this overflow occurred daily. Not imbibing before 5 p.m. was Arthur's idea of control. Interested in the subject of drinking personally and professionally, I had recently assisted a grad student friend teach a course called "Drugs and Alcohol in

American Society." I told Arthur then that under his condition of not discussing his drinking, we would never be more than boyfriend/girlfriend at best, never seriously committed, for however long. I made that vow to myself, knowing enough about people involved with heavy drinkers, such as my own mom, Betty, the wife of a bingeing man: my father, Jack.

Just coming off a year and a half long research project, a national study of domestic violence in the U.S, Arthur surprised me one time by choking me, as I mentioned, sitting atop me while I lay on his bed. In garbled syllables I told him I couldn't breathe to which he later responded, "Oh, I was just joking around." Really? He forgot to smile. In 2018, one of the former wives of Rob Porter, who was then a staffer in the Trump administration, accused Porter of that same behavior. Some commentators called it "strangling," to emphasize the danger of such aggressive behavior, suggesting "choking" minimized the act. For my part, Arthur rid me of a few bad habits: arguing with him in the morning when we were barely awake, and my own physical violence, throwing tissue boxes at the wall, and slamming doors, holdovers from my relationship with Charlie. He simply told me in a loud, forceful voice that these acts were unacceptable.

Of the stuff I left at his house, as far as I know, he still has an Art Deco vanity with a huge round mirror, and more importantly, my dad's army blanket from WWII.

A keepsake, the khaki-colored, all-wool covering kept us warm. Arthur protested when I wanted to remove it from the bed and take it with me, so I let him hold onto it, to my later regret. He said I could have the artist's proof of the mystery skelly scene that my brother owned, but I let that one go too, also to my lasting sorrow.

Soon after I moved, Arthur showed up as my guest at an academic shindig held near my college, driving in from over three hours away. He had turned down the opportunity to relocate with me, thinking the town too provincial, remarking that customers in a restaurant stared at him when he visited. Soon after his arrival, a faculty colleague who had grown up in an even smaller town stuck out his hand and said, "Hi, Don Josephs, Biology. Putting out his hand in return, Arthur said, "Hello, Arthur Allen, Cleveland." I chuckled, stifling a guffaw, though Professor Josephs didn't seem too amused. Interestingly, the two men had reached the same level of education, a Master's degree, the highest degree in Arthur's field, though not in Don's. I guess Arthur could have said, "Arthur Allen, Art." I would have laughed at that too, since those words didn't jibe with how he presented himself. He wouldn't have stated his identity in terms of a department or a field of study. He may have said, "Hi, I'm Arthur Allen. I'm an artist." He may have added, "I teach art."

Finding a couple of letters I had saved from Arthur reminded me that he thought I blamed him entirely for our problems, ranting on about how I didn't take any of the responsibility, which may have been at least partly true, looking back. I didn't push harder for laying out the issues and seeking resolution, even if it meant splitting up. Both of us blamed each other, not exactly a plan for success.

In these two undated letters written after periods of strained communication, Arthur stated he didn't understand why I "swing from mad to totally withdrawn," and from "not saying what's on your mind and getting too mad." But at the same time, Arthur admitted that he "may get confused, frustrated, and seemingly distant." He told me he was "as tired of our misunderstandings" as I was, not wanting to "risk a fight that goes in circles." And he finally wrote, "I'm sorry I'm not all you wish I would be."

Arthur mirrors my disappointment, about him and even more about the course of our relationship, in his last statement. It's an apology on its surface, yet not really, because he wouldn't regret who he is. Sounds to me like two people experiencing similar negative emotions, at a standstill. In these same notes, he also declared his love for me, words I believed but that seemed hollow, without any behavior that backed them up.

A final, memorable page I had kept for a while had Arthur's drawing of a gigantic screw, making me scratch my head at first. I asked someone else, a male friend, for interpretation. He came up with the literal "I got screwed," from Arthur's perspective. I came to read it as "Screw you," meaning me. I think Arthur confirmed the second reading. In either case, that screw likely represented the final nail (or screw) in the coffin of our relationship.

After I moved, our relationship died a slow and then not-so-slow death. I remember one day in my bed in the new place when Arthur said something that gave me the feeling that my side of the bed had sunk about two feet lower than the rest of the bed. Did you ever have that, the literal sinking feeling? It might have been a few minutes after Arthur told me he found a real leopard coat in the second-hand shop that he almost bought for me—but didn't. I love leopard print anything, fake or real, if it has black in with the caramel or gold and yellow tones. It looks good on me, I think, and I love the wildcat quality of the print. I still have a pair of leopard ears on a headband, purchased for Halloween one year. That's the only leopard skin thing I have now. Wait - actually - I kept my friend Damon's gift: an old girlfriend's fake leopard coat that I used to wear once in a while, such as to Las Vegas one winter. It has a spotted dog Scotty pin on the lapel made of tortoise-colored, translucent Bakelite. I sure would have loved a real leopard skin coat…

Near the very finish of our relationship, I had a local fling, a one-night stand with someone I acted in a play with, and mistakenly told Arthur. It was the last time I triggered a break-up by being unfaithful to someone. I phoned to ask him if I could come up to see him that New Year's Eve and he didn't answer. So I took a Greyhound bus up on Dec. 31st, calling him from the bus station. Turns out he had a date, or pretended to, anyway, and sent me home. He said, "You have to go home." I re-boarded the same bus, making the round trip back, looking out the large rear window. Through my tears, the window fog tempted me to write "The End" in large letters with my index finger, but I just held onto the thought. Bye-bye, Arthur. He ended up marrying someone who once went out with a close male friend of mine. My friend knew her to be a heavy drinker. I saw her once, a pretty redhead. She would not let me talk to Arthur, when I called his house, a few years after they married. "Who did you want? Whooo??" she asked repeatedly. I knew I had the right number.

Ow, I still have a dull ache inside my stomach, when I think about us, the potential of us. I had conceived an equalitarian partnership of an artist and a social scientist, a mix of intuition and rationality, music, art, and travel, optimistically, without the drinking, eventually. Once Arthur drove us over five hours to visit the headquarters of a Surrealist magazine in Chicago. There we discussed writing, art and culture with the editor in his office filled with images and press clippings. Ideally, I envisioned two people living out a blend of cosmopolitanism in the larger world and cozy domesticity at home. But I don't regret leaving him.

Interlude: "Like a Rolling Stone": Arthur Plays Dylan for Me

Very musical, Arthur could play the acoustic guitar and sing in that fulsome baritone he had. He plunked out Fats Waller's "I'm Gonna Sit Right Down and Write My Self a Letter" sitting on a chair in his living room, a favorite of mine. He taught me to like Leon Redbone, and to some degree, Patti Smith, whom we had seen in concert the day we met. Patti idolized the Stones and ultimately performed and recorded "Gimme Shelter" and other tunes of theirs. The Stones ended up covering Dylan's 1965 hit "Like a Rolling Stone" in the 90s, recording it in 1995. Crowds love it live, singing the chorus along with Mick at concerts, "...HOW does it FEE-EL?" "To be on your OWN." The audience almost shouts the title phrase as the song ends. Makes me tear up, to it hear in-person or recorded live versions, having grown up with it.

To the uninformed, "Like a Rolling Stone" seems named for the rock performers, though really lifted from the 1950 Muddy Waters tune "Rollin' Stone." Dylan appropriated its title, as Brian Jones had a few years earlier for the Rolling Stones band, and Jann Wenner for his magazine, Rolling Stone, two years after Dylan's song. With his wry English humor, Mick sometimes jokes when introducing it that "Now we'd like to do a song we wrote," or saying, instead, when Dylan opened for them in Rio de Janeiro, "a song that Bob Dylan wrote for us." At Night 1 of the Desert

Trip festival in 2016, Mick observed that his band had never before followed an opening act by a Nobel Prize winner, an honor recently bestowed on Dylan.

Arthur bought the album of Dylan's Slow Train Coming, *newly released around that time. To this day, I really like the title song, and another cut, "You've Got to Serve Somebody," even with the religious implications of the lyrics. Dylan wrote the album commemorating his concurrent conversion to evangelical Christianity from his upbringing in a kosher home, observing the traditions of Judaism. Dylan dropped his overt evangelism a few years later, reverting to a mix of theological and secular traditions more in line with most of his listeners, including Arthur and me.*

Chapter 5
"Beast of Burden":
Bobby the Superboy, the Momma's Boy

Bobby had a large sexual appetite, as in the song, "Beast of Burden"; he only wanted someone to make love with him, with endurance to match. Extremely strong because of his weightlifting, Bobby could carry heavy objects without strain, including me, on occasion. He could also eat a lot, downing three oversized cream puffs to win a restaurant contest, the filling spilling out as he munched. He also wanted to make his mark with his knowledge of Russian and his expertise with audio/visual materials, a path he built a career on. He had a dark sense of humor and probably wouldn't have minded serving as someone's literal "beast" because he liked to help people and organizations with physical tasks. Mick's description of the tune as an "attitude" song fits with Bobby's goal of serving well, internally questioning, following the song, if he is good enough or "rich enough" or "tough enough" to be an appropriate partner. Bobby was known to burst out with his talk/sung version of a different lyric: "Please baby, please, please, please," lifted from earlier blues and soul songs.

Possibly the love of my life, perhaps the last one, not counting Danny-boy, was Bobby, the weight lifter and long-distance runner. He resembled a shorter, stockier Superman in his sculptured yet delicate features and his Clark Kent-ish black horn-rimmed glasses sported before those square-ish heavy frames came back in style big-time. Replace the "black" hair of Christopher Reeve with the white-blond hair of Bobby, take off his glasses, and put him in a cape or suit, and there he was, Lois Lane's boyfriend, or maybe Superboy, a younger version. Bobby had more of the demeanor as well as the glasses and the lack of self-confidence of Clark Kent, with a stooped posture much of the time. I once bought him a Ralph Lauren periwinkle blue Polo shirt but his arms threatened to bust open the seams so he had to return it. He enjoyed people looking at him, much more than I did, often playing the exhibitionist to my voyeur. In an ad we noticed in a magazine for a candy product at Easter, he identified with the white rabbit with the bright bow, a female bunny, whereas I was the brown one in canvas hat and sunglasses, the male, hiding. We chuckled at the reversal of traditional genders.

Bobby liked PDA and I usually enjoyed it to the extent that clothing stayed in place. Soon after we met, he exclaimed happily that he enjoyed my affectionate nature, my receptivity to receiving and giving physical contact. We were huggy bears, all right, even fondly addressing each other as "Bear," both using the name, with a capital "B." The funny part is when he was mad at me or frustrated, he used the same name, with a sour tone, drawn out: "Be-eaaaaar!"

He expressed interest in me for two reasons, I think, first because I was an academic, a faculty member, supposedly of some intelligence. He told me I was probably "the smartest woman" he had known, which I took as a compliment, the best he could do. Then there was my anatomy, an accident of genetics, inherited from my mother, these large breasts, sprouted since my adolescence, rarer before implants were all that common. I didn't know how serious he was about this interest, until he told me of a magazine he regularly purchased subtitled "Home of the G cup." Skeptical, he showed it to me on a local magazine rack. I think he already had the most recent issue. He sometimes pointed out a woman with sizable breasts to tell me he liked her, even if she carried excess poundage aside from the mammaries. We had a receptionist like that at our workplace and he joked he could slide down her breasts, since she could fit two or three of him on the front of her body.

Bobby's mom Penny worked with us in the same building, part of the complex of the regional university. A personable woman, she held those proverbial apron strings close, tied tightly around her still-trim waist. Remarkable to me, and at least slightly enviable, since my childhood did not contain such attention, she labeled his paper lunch bags daily, with his name, "BOBBY," hand-printed in capital letters on them, in black marker. He was the only child left at home, and as far as I know, her husband ate lunch in his work cafeteria. My mom rarely packed a brown bag for me, and when she did, say for a grade school trip, it sat unnamed in the fridge overnight. She did iron nametags into my underwear over the brand name for sleep-away camp so that no one mistook me, however unlikely, for "Calvin Klein" as happened to Marty McFly in *Back to the Future*.

An athlete into adulthood, Bobby had extended his marathon runs from high school through his recent daily treks, much shorter than the 26-mile races he competed in then. He weight-lifted, influenced as a pre-teen by the Charles Atlas ads on the ninety-pound weakling turned strong man, narrowly escaping building his muscles too much for my taste. His legs in his running shorts looked very good, nicely shaped and smooth. An Arnold Schwarzenegger poster graced one wall of his bedroom at home. Did I mention he still lived with his parents in his late twenties? Granted the location of their house let him commute a very short distance to his job, where we both worked. A fun demonstration of his strength that happened in the spring one year had Bobby lifting me up on his back and running down the main street in the German Village neighborhood of Columbus, Ohio. I yelled happily,

"Yippee," as if he was my very own horsey taking me for a ride. The ride went on for a long block before I asked to come down. It reminded me of how my dad used to put me on his shoulders as a kid and trot me around, mainly indoors.

On the up side too, Bobby had a generous bent—he would give away just about anything. This tendency sometimes went in strange directions, not always to my benefit. Three weeks after we began seeing each other, I left on a scheduled trip out of state for a conference. When I returned, my car was gone. Bobby admitted he had lent it to a friend of his, who hadn't brought it back. Worse yet, when I insisted that he find the friend to bring the car back, Bobby found my tone of voice upsetting. Red flag, waving wildly, in hindsight? Another time, he had bought me some free weights, two each in the three, five, and ten-pound sizes. Walking past a colleague's office, I saw what looked like the same three pair sitting in a corner near the desk. I asked the professor, "Excuse me, where did you get those?" He answered, "From Bobby." I checked at home later in the day to find them missing, as I had suspected. As soon as I told the current possessor that I believed those to be my weights, a present, he agreed to hand them over, horrified.

When approaching his car, Bobby would make a 360-degree turn, arms out, feet close together. Answering my query as to "What is this?" he said he merely wanted to ensure no bystanders wanted to jump him or take his property. I later learned that this could make the list of many symptoms of the alcoholic or the recovering alcoholic. I went to many AA meetings with Bobby, encountering those who would accuse me of being an alcoholic or ask me, "Are you sure you're not the alcoholic?" between the two of us, instead of the friend or family member. I concluded they felt that because I was more outgoing, and indeed, more likely to show irritation in public. Much later, at an Adult Children of Alcoholics meeting, I found out that many of us close to alcoholics adopt their characteristics, even without drinking at all.

These AA people who challenged me, all men, suspected that my volatility and extroversion matched better with the alcoholic personality than Bobby's outward politeness and willingness to serve. Behind closed doors, in the house or in the car, Bobby would call me names or accuse me of blocking his will. Once he reached for an appellation for me while spinning the car in circles in a parking lot, sputtering, "You..... you......you.....slut!" Stifling a laugh, I said, "What do you mean by that?" since I was only seeing one man then, him. I recited the Serenity Prayer in the car under my breath, a practice that would come in handy for any upset in everyday life.

For a while, we had the same therapist, Alfred, the psychologist, just down the street from work, very convenient. Delivering the A/V equipment to my classroom one day, Bobby had something on his mind: "Alfred told me what you said about me," embodying my nightmare. You know, right, that if a therapist will violate the confidentiality of a client, that relationship is over? In this case, it should never have started. By repeating what I had said about him to Bobby, Alfred had violated one of the basic rules of treatment. Yes, maybe I tempted Alfred by telling him Bobby had been less than honest with Alfred, but still. I may have purposely tested him, I wondered later, or else I was just pissed off that Alfred didn't know the truth. In either case, the situation contained the seeds of conflict from its beginning. Betrayed, I never again sought therapy, trying this last time many years after I briefly went to a couple of therapists during my marriage to Charlie.

The first hint of Bobby's capacity for physical violence came when he pounded on his car's hood, which I thought signaled a conscious channeling of his rage to denting objects instead of humans. I mentioned that to him and he nodded, not commenting. However, one time, while parked inside the car in front of our school, he told me to hit him as hard as I could. At first I told him no, recalling Houdini's serious rumored death from a boy under the same circumstances. Lying back on a couch, with no chance to brace himself for the four blows to his abdomen, he suffered pain and could not sleep. Houdini died not too long after his fan's visit. Before his death he had a ruptured appendix removed, postponing the operation to do a show the night before, complicating the diagnosis of cause of his demise. Bobby hadn't heard Houdini's story, insisting I go ahead and sock him in the stomach. After taking a couple of hits, saying "Harder," before the second one, he suddenly slapped me, with enough force to sting. We never tried that game again.

A worse scene came at his parents' house where he lived and stayed when he wasn't at my place, when his mom Penny was home, on a weekend. Bobby's mom, Bobby, and me formed another one of those triads in my life. I didn't discover that right away. In the living room watching TV, she had indicated to Bobby that she wanted to accompany us to the movies, a request I quietly denied when Bobby and I talked in the kitchen. The next thing I knew he pushed me hard, to the floor. His mother called out, "What's the matter?" I denied that anything was wrong, not knowing what to say.

Triggering one of our break-ups, she called him to demand that he come home that evening to take care of their plants, while she and Bobby's dad vacationed elsewhere. Bobby and I had planned for him to stay the weekend at my two-story apartment in German Village. He felt he would have to comply, and also knew how serious our plans were. After a few minutes of listening to my side, he went to lie down on his stomach in the carpeted bedroom, limbs akimbo, as if to embody the tug of war, his mother and me each metaphorically pulling on one leg, as if he was a wishbone. Cr-aa-aa-aaa-ck! He already knew his mother had won—well, anyway, she got the bigger half. I knew she had won, and would always win, as far as I could tell at that moment.

As noted, Bobby and I were involved together in the 12-step programs, me going to both "open" AA meetings, those not closed to non-alcoholics, along with my own Al-Anon or children of alcoholics meetings. Always curious about how this world-wide self-help group began after a stockbroker and a doctor met in Akron, Ohio, I read much of AA's literature, and briefly considered doing a study on male Al-Anons, men whose partners were, primarily, female alcoholics. I dropped the idea when I didn't find more than a few, hearing that most of those guys left their spouses with drinking problems, unlike many of the women married to male alcoholics.

We attended the 50th Anniversary convention of Alcoholics Anonymous in Montreal, where the city officials opened up free subway rides for everyone, what with 60,000 new people in town. We heard Lois Wilson, the wife of AA's co-founder Bill W speak and a founder herself of Al-Anon: what a thrill. Bobby and I took a chartered bus up there with other recovering people from Ohio. Our problems heightened with the travel to a far-away metropolis, a city in a different country where French was the native and much preferred language. He didn't enjoy waking up early and getting out and about, as I did. At one point, frustrated about something, he threw his papers and books on the ground, in the midst of a fairly crowded area. I stood a few feet away as more than one person from "the program" asked me, "Are you okay?" So sweet, if embarrassing. I assured them I was, while Bobby fumed, his body language and facial expressions communicating his still-simmering anger and frustration, as he retrieved his objects. Some people would have called that the behavior of a "dry drunk," someone sober in a superficial sense, but not yet living well, not following the twelve steps.

We had, what was for us, a funny moment or two, listening to the "leads," the speakers talking about the depths of where they came from, and how they got out of their addiction and into recovery. A few of these people were nationally known for their ability to galvanize crowds with humor and pathos. One time, we were arguing loudly in the stadium just before the founder's wife Lois W took the microphone to speak, someone we wanted to hear. Bobby, holding a cake donut, went to take a bite of it when it broke off, half of it dropping into his paper cup full of coffee. We found that hilarious in the moment, both cracking up, leaving the conflict aside, as the tender donut piece fell—ker-plop! It didn't take a lot for us to laugh in those days. We shared a dark sense of humor that goes with growing up in a dysfunctional home, with the idea that we'd rather laugh than cry.

On the ride home, he took a different seat, with no room for me to sit with him. I asked another passenger if

I could exchange seats, to sit next to an unresponsive, stone-faced Bobby. On the trip there, we were called "the lovebirds," closing ourselves in the bathroom for privacy time, and now he wasn't even talking to me. When I returned home, I remember I was, by far, more seriously suicidal than I've ever been. Bobby had frozen me out of any communication with him. Someone from the program told me to come to a meeting in my upset, and I've said that going there saved my life. That's how I felt at the time, anyway, with no concrete plans on how I would've offed myself. Not a vengeful person, not in my behavior, usually, I had a small stuffed figure that I turned into a voodoo doll, tentatively sticking a few pins into my little felt Bobby. Hmm, about a week later, when we finally talked on the phone, he said, "I hurt my arm with my tools when I was up on the roof, trying to fix it." I didn't tell him about my black magic doll, trying not to laugh out loud. Not serious, his wound was superficial. I surmised he had become more uncoordinated in the aftermath of our bus trip, maybe from worry and lack of sleep, but hey, you never know. We got back together, continuing a cycle that went on for a while, break-up, make-up, break-up, make-up.

Bobby flirted with both men and women and had even been involved with one man regularly. In the age of AIDS I told him he had to give that one up, as I wrote a paper on the changing portrayal of AIDS in the media, national attention increasing right after Rock Hudson announced he had it. "He must have had a blood transfusion," said my mom, refusing to believe such a hunk, an idol, this tall, dark and handsome paramour of Doris Day could be gay. That was when I memorized the Serenity Prayer, especially helpful in the car with Bobby, where he would rant endlessly about this or that, always my fault. "Accept the things I cannot change" was a particularly potent line that stays with me to this day. But I was still obsessed with Bobby and couldn't leave yet. Our theater director, seeing us together in the hallway, told me to invite Bobby to a rehearsal since, if I haven't made that clear yet, "I only had eyes for him," a paraphrase of the lyrics from the 1934 song by Harry Warren and Al Dubin introduced in the film *Dames*, a hit for The Flamingos in 1959.

During my tenure case, as I call the period of my life when I wasn't sure I would keep my job or stay in academia, the focus of my life for some twenty years until that point, Bobby became agitated about the unfairness of the judgments made against me, by people on my committee, all outside of my field. While not disagreeing with him, my goal was to see if I could keep my job, which to me meant if not hiding out, then not making waves. On the other hand, Bobby was more about self-expression or rather, holding his anger in until it burst out full-blown. He helped me stoke the fires of resentment, a primary emotion AA advises against. At one point he became a barrier to my progressing with my career at least in the job I held.

The Vice-Provost decided to throw me out of my office after I consulted people "over his head," the first time I was tossed from a living or office space since my late adolescence. I had to move out all my books, papers and personal furniture, after nearly a decade of accumulation. Bobby had taken boxes out for me to put in a truck to take back home to Columbus. A kind colleague across the hall told me he would keep an eye on the office, holding it for me until I returned, he imagined, after winning my case. Bobby did not take the Vice-Provost's edict lightly. Much like he had done with his belongings in Montreal at the AA conference he started throwing my books around, in front of the entrance to the main building of two on our campus, this time yelling something about how it wasn't fair, about the tenure case, using unpleasant names for the faculty on the committee. I talked him down out of the fit, thinking what have I done here? At that point, I knew I had to prepare to give him up. He was risking my job's future, or "maybe, just maybe," one of Bobby's favorite phrases, my relationship with him was at least part of the reason I found myself the first person in the regional campus' history to face denial of tenure.

Among the professors who didn't care for him was the chair of my tenure and promotion committee, Donald, who often saw Bobby in the gym. He had told me I should not see Bobby at all, stating a conflict of interest. Since Bobby was a staff member and never my student and neither of us had any authority to affect the other's evaluations, the head honcho of our campus later told me he would have quashed the command from the committee chair if I had reported it earlier. Donald had also once commented on my apparel, stating he didn't believe women should wear boots with skirts (!). Another man on the committee who engineered my defeat, Evan, had maintained a clandestine affair with Bobby's mother, a liaison between two married people. Evan understood that I would know about it through Bobby though I didn't care. Evan was divorced not long after. Bobby and I agreed without much discussion that the other two just carried the third guy, Franklin, with them. Franklin was a professor in a technical field unrelated to the social sciences, and relatively uninterested in the case and clueless about the process. On a personal note, Franklin had tried to become Bobby's pal, with Bobby spending much less time with him when I came along. He was none too fond of me for supposedly coming between him and Bobby. Three out of three disliked at least one of us coming into the situation, hmmm, not a promising outlook.

Taking a lie detector test, Bobby submitted his answers as evidence to those adjudicating my appeal that the committee member, Evan, and his mother had dallied for some time. He hoped that the paper stating the truthfulness of his answers would prove bias in my case by the local committee. Whether it played a role or not, I never would know. I like to think the merits of the case spoke strongly in my favor on the quality of my teaching, scholarship and service. I had asked Bobby if he made clear that I had nothing to do with his decision go into the examiner and get all wired up, or to make the results available to the appeals committee. In the meantime, Bobby also privately threatened to take an ax to both Donald's and Evan's doors.

During this time, one night, I had a *dream*:

It was a courtroom. I was on trial. The judge sat atop a huge chair behind a giant podium made of dark wood, perhaps mahogany, or perhaps walnut. I noticed the massive block of wood more than its particular grain or exact color. The whole judge's platform must have been about twelve feet high off the ground. The judge and his assistants perched up there, one on either side of him, with groups of onlookers sitting in bleacher-like booths attached to the left and right walls of the narrow space containing my trial. In imitation of one of my favorite books, the dream emulated features of *Alice in Wonderland*, when Alice changed size. Everyone except me seemed larger and louder than life. It was as if I had eaten a bite of cake that shrunk me, or in the words of the Jefferson Airplane, "one pill makes you larger, and one pill makes you small." Here is what the judge and his cohorts told me, with my responses, as best as I can recall, slightly enhanced for conscious comprehension:

Judge: What are you thinking, putting all your emotion into your relationship? Don't you know what you're doing? You could lose your job permanently.

Cohorts: Yes, what's up? What's going on? Are you crazy?

Me: I know, I know.

Judge: You know, if you continue acting this way, I will be forced to sentence you to a lifetime of boring jobs, with almost no time off and cretins for co- workers.

Cohorts: Hear, hear, a dreary life for you.

Me: Oh, dear. What can I do?

Judge: Drop this guy like a red-hot potato, and do it now, no second thoughts! Get your priorities in order. This is your life.

Cohorts: Get rid of him. Tell him to get lost.

Me: Okay, we're pretty much split up now anyway, and have broken up before, so it shouldn't be too hard to make the final break. I guess this is it, huh?

Judge: (*banging his huge gavel three times, making a thunderous, pounding sound*):

Guilty as charged on three counts: relationship hoarding, fear of letting go, and avoidance of being alone!! Penalty is many years of existing without a main man in your life.

Assistants: Hear, hear! (*vigorously nodding and raising their arms high in agreement*)

Cohorts: No men! No interference! No takeovers of who you are or what you do!

Me: Okay, okay.

Waiting a moment before departing, I half-expected to hear "off with her head," and when that didn't happen, I woke up, knowing what I had to do. I had never had such clear, direct admonitions in a dream, advice that I had already just about taken, if still questioning it a little, maybe wishfully thinking all the problems would pass.

Bobby and I were off again, almost for good this time, after he came banging on my apartment door demanding to get in, with the results of his lie detector test. I let him hang out there, refusing to open the door. In the later stages, Bobby told his friend in front of me, "I almost married her." I thought, "You did?" We reunited for a few weeks when he was becoming serious about his new girlfriend. We knew it was a final test of "us." We started taking Sunday walks, and he also showed me the new house his parents had built for him in a subdivision. He said, "This could have been yours." After a while, even with an ongoing attraction, we began arguing heavily. Around then, his girlfriend decided she had enough of our walks, forbidding Bobby to see me anymore. Good thing, I thought, admiring her gumption.

While Bobby and I never saw the Stones live, he did appreciate their music, and supported my love for it. During the last, mostly-off stage with Bobby, I went to see the Stones for the first time with a former student who took me to two shows in Ohio. In Cincinnati, sitting fairly close up, my friend told me he identified with Keith Richards, while he played air guitar along with Keith's real one. He noticed I seemed to relate more to Mick. Yessir! I imitated him once at a party in Costa Rica when the host played a Rolling Stones CD. I joined in with an artist I knew from our arts residency who mimicked Keith, grabbing a broom for a guitar. I was hooked on their live shows forever after, following them to Las Vegas in the MGM Grand with its pristine sound and talking my brother into going with me in Chicago. For a later tour, I had fifth row aisle seats and soon attracted Mick's attention by my intense focus on him, and standing up when not everyone did. I yelped with joy when he started his harmonica in "Can't You Hear Me Knocking," my favorite tune. To my surprise, he motioned that he would get back to me later, returning to offer direct, extensive eye contact.

After we split for good, Bobby's mom Penny apologized to me for clutching him so close for so long. He was living with the new girlfriend by then, in the house Bobby's parents had bought. She wanted me to hang out with her, but I couldn't, since my feelings for her son had not yet burned down to coals. Her remorse reminded me of similar regrets from my aunt, my mom's sister-in-law and best friend, who told me many years later that she felt sorry she had interfered in my relationship with her son, my cousin, when we were in junior high and lived only a few blocks from each other. He and I are still close today.

When I called Bobby a few times in the years after, he yelled at me, still upset about the tenure stuff, still talking about how badly the faculty had treated me, still calling me "Bear," in the midst of his angry talk.

Interlude: "Can You Hear the Music:" Bobby and the Blues Band:

Unasked, Bobby bought the Stones album "Some Girls." I played it and loved it. He took me to hear the Paul Butterfield Blues Band, after my friend the harmonica player advised me to see them while I still could, in their later days. Wow! They weren't fast, but they were tight and really captured the essence of the Chicago blues style, first emerging from artists such as Muddy Waters and Howlin' Wolf. Written by Nick Gravenites, "Born in Chicago" captured the angst and mayhem of a life style of old and new blues players, featuring Paul Butterfield' gritty voice and superb harmonica, one of my favorite instruments. Butterfield turns soulful for the ballad "Driftin' and Driftin' by Charles Brown singing of love lost, a man left alone, floating at sea. Bobby and I both adored The Blues genre, the basis for the beginnings of The Rolling Stones, considered a blues band before they began writing blues-rock tunes of their own. At the Butterfield show, I sat on his lap and we cuddled, in our affectionate "Bear" mood, fueled by the music.

Chapter 6
"Dancing with Mr. D":
Danny the Dog, Player of Women and Guitars

I once asked Danny if he thought he was the guy our mothers had warned us about, and he said, "Oh, yeah." Consorting with him, aware of his infidelities, was like taking up with the devil, Mr. D, the subject of the song. At his house, as I started to move to the rock music coming from his speakers, he once asked, "Wanna dance for me, baby?" Huh, sure: "Dancing with Mr. D": Danny the Dog. And Danny routinely expected several females to dance at the front of the bandstands where he played bass in various local bands, some of whom would offer to take him home after the show. When with Danny, stoned on sex and marijuana and music, I was temporarily carefree, until I had to leave for work or go home to the cats. We spent hours in his den, feeling like we were back in the 70's, entering the wayback machine to live in the counterculture, like the hippies of yore.

A man with the same nickname as his dog. Really?

Yes, they were both "Lucky Dog": the dog, and his human also known by me as "Dog" or "Lucky," if I felt particularly affectionate, or by his given name, "Danny." Dog and man, animals, both. This person might have been the wildest of my sex maniac men. He wants to dress me up, okay; he wants to dress me down, sure, fine; he wants to make movies of the two of us having sex; I'm game, as long as they stay between us. This was, of course, before phone or online videos became common. Wait, he wants to do what, now?

Mmmm…no.

Speaking on the phone at the very beginning of our several-year liaison, auspiciously initiated by his online ad, Danny told me he felt a spark. When we met, that spark, the frisson, was definitely there. He was a bass player in a soft rock band, a side gig to his day job as a telephone customer service rep. For a period in the late 1970's into the 1980's, he had played lead guitar and keyboards full-time in a popular local band, making a living at it. At a concert, I heard his acquaintance call him "a monster guitar player." I admired people with musical ability and the presence to play in front of audiences. He noticed that I pulled on his belt at his house, a provocative gesture, he felt, that I did almost unconsciously. My behavior indicated both a powerful physical attraction to him, and that I felt free enough to act on it. I had already known that he was a longhaired, mustachioed musician from his ad, where he carried his instrument as if playing it, wearing aviator shades and a white shirt. A couple of years later, I showed the ad to my brother, the male arbiter in my life, to let him know about Danny. He said, "Wow," impressed, or he acted like he was, a reaction that I took as a kind of approval.

Later, when I decided to investigate the origin of all the conflicts between Danny and me, I re-read his ad, and saw something that as a student of online relationships should have made him an immediate "no". Apparently, I let my reptile brain slide past what his ad actually was for: he wasn't looking for a girlfriend. He was looking for a band-mate — female. Turns out he already had a girlfriend.

This female intimate had instituted a rule that Danny had to save weekends for her, before and after and in place of any gigs with a band he might have scheduled. While she wasn't the mother of his beloved daughter, his only child who was living on her own at first, (the third party with me and Danny in another triad, in addition to the one with his girlfriend,) they had been involved for a long time. Danny wouldn't tell me how long. The pain I felt during our separations on the weekend and during much of the week derived more from him not seeing me than from him seeing another woman, and that Danny kept our relationship a secret.

Describing himself the first time we met offline as like the Tom Hanks' character in *Big*, I knew later I should have paid more attention to that film rather than half-watching it online with a friend who actually wanted to see it. Researching our relationship issues further, I recalled that Danny said he had the emotional maturity of a 12-year-old boy. Oh, that's funny, I thought, chuckling. Danny then added, "Well, maybe an 8-year-old." So really, less than twelve. I was to learn more about the implications of that statement in the months and years to come.

From the get-go, Danny and I always seemed to have trouble connecting. Before we met in person, I had problems with my computer while on a writing stint in another state, and we lost contact. I read his messages expressing sadness that we weren't connecting, and my non-working technology stifled my usual quick-trigger responses, making me seem distant. I tried to arrange for a meeting at an Eric Clapton concert we were both attending, but he didn't read my message on the dating site in time. I had an usher look for him. The next day he replied in email that he would have showed up on the stairs, had he seen my note, suggesting we connect in person soon. Another time, shortly after we talked at his house in "real life," I sat in a bar alone during the daytime for over an hour, waiting for him to show up. Before everyone had cell phones, we had few means of communicating our moment-to-moment whereabouts.

After that caper—he said he had been "held up"—I vowed not to meet him again outside of one of our homes, except for once or twice at the coffee house I frequented to use the internet.

Besides our physical intimacy—more about that later— we also had fun times hearing familiar, loved music, and introducing the other (mostly him introducing me) to new, unknown music. We had a playful, creative relationship, with musical and artistic elements, and word play. In line with my longtime love of voice, we sang the theme from "The Mickey Mouse Club," me on melody, him harmonizing on the spelled-out word "M-O-U-S-EEE." He discovered a cartoon app, "Comic Life," sending me a one panel, two-character thought. I extended that to a whole storyboard between a man and a woman, with a plot, simple as it was, complete with background, conflict, and resolution. Going back and forth designing the panels, we imagined the characters looked like us, voicing our sentiments. He played the guitar for me a few times, and sang, original tunes and old favorites. When we went to concerts together, our mutual appreciation ran deep. Standing near the front of the stage at an outside show of the master guitarist Eric Johnson playing the melodic "Cliffs of Dover," which had won a Grammy for best rock instrumental, Danny announced in a wry understatement, "I guess I need to work on my tone."

Danny liked words, as I do, but had found higher education too boring to hold his attention or to invest his limited funds. Like Arthur, he sometimes made up words when the ordinary word felt inexpressive. He liked to say "mayhaps," a combination of "maybe" and "perhaps," derived from an Old English word "mayhap," a shortened form of "may happen."

Being called by a nickname has always felt affectionate or outright loving to me. Today I am known by most as "Andee," transformed in spelling from my childhood name of "Andi," short for the full name, "Andrea." People I've liked have called me that, with the exception of a few years when I went by my full name inside academia. My ex Charlie liked my full name, whereas a friend from that time always called me by my nickname. Bobby and I had spontaneously coined "Bear," maybe off our childhood time spent cuddling our Teddy bears. Some people like to rename others with variations of their names, including my brother who named one of my cousins Ned, "the Nedster," and another cousin he called "J/K," two initials, after her name change confused us for a while. I like to call Joel "my little baby brother" or "bro-bee," to his face. Danny just liked to address me with affectionate words that could apply to many women, such as "darlin'," or more rarely, "baby doll." I interpret that as a verbal hug, and also connect it to blues singers such as Stevie Ray Vaughan who wrote "Pride and Joy" about a paramour, his "sweet little baby."

Okay, let's get down to the literal juice of the Lucky Dog tale, the liquids emitted by the body: the messy yet necessary parts of the sexual act. Years before meeting Danny, after I had gone through menopause, I had a brief, nasty encounter with a man who accused me of lacking moisture. Even with an applied lubricant, the "act" just wasn't going to work. I asked my gynecologist for estrogen pills, which I took for a while, until the studies of the side effects made that alternative unrealistic: too risky in the doctor's view. Then I heard about the vaginal ring, a device you insert that releases small amounts of hormones, that was supposed to be safer. That seemed to work okay until Danny and I finally went "all the way," and then he complained that he bumped into it in the process. We decided to take it out, with him helping me...what a sight that must have been, almost worse than close-up scenes from a doctor's office, only with me half kneeling backwards on his bed. Reaaaaaaach...no, not quite. Try again...a little higher...almost...one more time...ah, okay, he got it.

His reasoning was that I didn't really need extra moisture, evidenced by the copious fluids flowing out when he touched me for a while. That seemed to make sense, and did ever after, with him, anyway, reinforcing my thought that it's primarily the partner and the quality of communication not the biology that reigns when determining sexual turn-ons. He taught me - through trying different techniques - more about what I liked, remembering which ones worked well for me and which ones didn't.

Talking of turn-ons, this human dog committed two acts I wouldn't have thought would inspire me sexually. First, and I hear this is common today, he sent me an explicit photo of his penis, which he called his "cock". Ordinarily, if you asked me, I would have denied finding that attractive, but in this case, somehow I did. He was taking a chance. What if I would have found the unrequested picture lewd, unspeakably gross, and a reason, pardon the expression, to cut off the relationship, such that it was? When I think back on it, the black and white photo had the quality of a sculpture, with its myriad of grey tones. He told me a friend took it. It had an appealing shape and size, smooth, like an obelisk, less abstract toward its top. Then the other act happened when we walked in my neighborhood. He ran his fingers gently inside my waistband, down into the nether region and just fiddled around down there. With a few strokes he proved himself a master of his borrowed instrument, as if he played a rare and delicate tune on this particular body part, tuned to his (and my) satisfaction. I thought to myself, and told him this later, "Wow, this guy knows what he is doing. Holy cow." Maybe it was due to all those years using his fingers as a bass and keyboard player, or equally likely, on all the women he had known and mostly lost. Whatever it was, it was new to me. For me, he was unparalleled in expertise. I knew then that I was in big trouble. Whatever his faults, he had me in his spell, you know, "that old black magic."

Danny Lucky Dog brought me to orgasm almost all of the time. This process became shorter as my body got used to such release, but he wanted me to have two or three to every one of his. Acquiescing to my preferences, his hands rather than his mouth stimulated me gently yet persistently, employing a kind of butterfly technique, back and forth, not too hard or soft, adjusting his touch to my nonverbal reactions. This meant postponing his own climaxes, which he did through a combination of holding back, and, a unique prospect to me, a repertoire of cock rings. I watched curiously as he opened their special case, and then he slid one or the other or a combination of these down to the base of his penis. The rings were either made of metal or silicone, I'm not sure. These aids apparently enhanced his ability to retard his ejaculation, while I didn't feel them at all. Another tactic of his was to remove his underwear early on, taking off his Jockeys without taking off his shirt, once he knew I was with him on the sex journey. That took me off guard at first. To me the usual sequence when undressing the other person or oneself is to remove the layers above the waist before those below. I came to see it as a playful move, reminding me of when toddlers pulled off their diapers or underpants, running around happily, without shame, while their parents laughed. The other men I knew almost as free with nudity were Bobby, proud of his body, and Sam, who once visited me wearing nothing under his long coat, and also took us up on the roof of a university building, before someone complained after hearing the sounds we made.

Once, Danny, after asking me if it was okay, velcroed my hands to hooks at the top of a closet door, effectively immobilizing me during sex. *Fifty Shades of Grey*, anyone? He gave me hickeys at first, stopping after I objected, saying the obvious marks on my neck were not a good look for work. The venture I chickened out of involved a real-life man Danny found on an online site who wanted to have sex with the two of us, and his wife, each couple watching the other online, maybe to meet offline later. Luckily the man's wife refused to come out of their upstairs bedroom. My own demurral seemed to agree with her assessment of the situation. I remember sitting next to Danny, fully clothed, looking into the screen at this guy available for sex with strangers, feeling a mix of distance, disinterest, and fear that Danny would try to pressure me into the scenario. After my response, he never mentioned that possibility again.

An anecdote from his much younger days had him pleasuring one woman in a bedroom while another paramour, unaware of the activities upstairs talked with other company outside. The only problem was that Danny and his female bedmate were having so much fun that the woman with him screamed his name in ecstasy, "Danny, oh, Danny," the words drifting out through the open windows. I'm glad I never put myself in that circumstance, around Danny and other women in houses not our own.

About his girlfriend… In the beginning, he intimated they might split up soon. I knew better than to believe that. Later in our relationship, driving somewhere together, I told him I was upset with him about his other relationship. He answered, "Andee, a lot of men my age have girlfriends." What? OMG. What am I then? The mistress to the girlfriend or the second girlfriend or…? Not as important, that's for sure, I thought. He didn't really give a definitive answer, mumbling apparent agreement with me when I suggested maybe I was girlfriend number two. Neither of us had Mormon relatives. He had suggested I meet girlfriend number one, without identifying to her, my relationship to him. I declined.

One part of Danny that was so enticing from the start was his knowledge of a woman's body, as I already indicated. I had become addicted to the sex, as well as to his voice, and his smell. Once he gave me an unwashed t-shirt that I kept next to my pillow until the odor wore off. I never asked him exactly how many women he had slept with. I'm guessing it was a three-digit number. He had devoted himself to supplementing his long-term partnerships with a constant stream of one-night stands or short-term lovers, both during more steady relationships and in-between them. The downside of this for some of his partners meant a clear lack of commitment to even the concept of monogamy, The positive here pointed to the best lover I would ever have, or at least the most skilled and patient sexual partner I had met up to this point. Be careful what you wish for. When I asked him how long he had ever been faithful to one person, he said maybe several months, definitely less than a year. I cried a lot during our so-called relationship, more than over any other man, especially when he would cancel out on a planned encounter.

Another man known for his dalliances and sexual charisma, Mick Jagger's two wives, and other girlfriends put up with a massive amount of infidelity. His second wife Jerry, divorced him finally when he fathered a child outside of their union, with his extra-marital Brazilian partner. Mick has said he is not suited for marriage, never wedding his long-time, live-in partner L'Wren of twelve years, before her suicide. Danny never wanted to marry, and only had one child, compared to Mick's eight, from five different women.

After I knew he had a serious partner, something he told me almost right away, I rarely talked about him to anyone during our several years of seeing each other. Except in the inner, overly romantic recesses of my mind, I didn't take seriously his caveat that they weren't getting along well and might break up soon. Danny and

I were both in our late 50s or early 60s then, and though he was a few years younger, we were both plenty old enough to know something of life and yet apparently young enough to still be surprised by what a new person could bring into our worlds. My closest friend, Hope, didn't want to hear about him, defining our relationship as purely a booty call, something she never ever would engage in. Also, one of her ex-husbands had been unfaithful, wounding her, understandably. My little brother would say, if I mentioned him, "Are you still seeing that guy?"

Towards the end, our physical intimacy, other than a few hugs, had largely stopped, because his daughter moved back in with him and because I didn't want to have sex with him in my own house, undependable as he was. He came over and sat down on the couch next to me, holding a jump drive. He inserted the drive into my computer to download its contents.

"I want you to hear this song I wrote."

"Okay."

I listened and had an inkling of its possible subject.

"I like it".

"You should. It's about you."

"Oh, really," I thought. Danny was on vocals and

guitar. The song, called "'Til Evening Comes," had a male narrator writing about his female paramour. When I heard he wrote it for me, I had that feeling you get when you think you're dreaming because your dreams are coming true. The song finishes with these lines:

Stay with me now baby,

Stay with me 'til morning comes

Stay with me now darlin',

Stay until forever comes

Two deaths occurred during the time I knew Danny: his mom's and his dog's. I never met his mother, but I felt sympathy for him: he was her only child, her son. With the dog, on the other hand, I myself felt a real loss. Up to that point I had only known a few dogs well in my life, and he was one of the finest. He was large and gentle, some sort of a Shepherd mix who ran towards you in welcome so fast you were scared, and then gracefully slowed to a stop, inches from you, hardly skidding at all. We would have to kick him out of bed to make room for ourselves. He would sleep in the nearby hallway and his legs would twitch during his doggy dreams. One day when Danny came over without Lucky, I asked where he was. Danny said he didn't take car trips much anymore, and then, not too long after that, I asked about him again, and Danny said he was no more. After his death, I missed that dog, almost as much as I later missed Danny, maybe more.

Eventually, our time together ended, mainly because I moved to a different state, and after that, his girlfriend of many years passed away of longtime health complications. Her obituary listed Danny as her "longtime companion." That gave me a pang, in the heart region. He had said we would get together if and when she died. Cold, huh? Somehow, I thought that would never happen: her death or us becoming primary partners. I was right. I had the lyrics to the song "'Til Evening Comes" put into a collaged work, a painting an artist did for me, along with some words from my writing on online relationships. I couldn't bring myself to put a picture of the dog in it, much less the man, but I did have a bunch of postage stamps of a head shot of Lucky made up, most of which I still have… Good ol' Lucky Dog. The canine was perhaps the sweetest part, certainly the most dependable, of my time with Danny. He would lay there close to the bed, sharing the sexual afterglow with the two us, the peace before sleep.

Interlude: "Love is Strong:" Watching the Band

Danny never went to a Stones show with me, although we did watch some of their videos and listened to a lot of old blues music from an internet radio station. We saw BB King and John Hammond Jr., but walked out on an outdoor show of Buddy Guy's when he left the stage to let his backup band play for a good 45 minutes. Danny and I once tuned in to catch The Rolling Stones do a couple of tunes on a live music awards show on TV, when they were a bit off their game. Mick occasionally glanced at his guitar playing band-mates, appearing to ask, along with us, "What the fuck is going on?" when he heard a few obviously off-key chords. Hoping to show off "my band" to Danny, I was embarrassed for them.

Chapter 7
"Memory Motel":
Miscellaneous Men

Here I use this song metaphorically to group these men into a building, a house, a motel, made of memories, although ironically, the one I never had sex with was the only one to suggest first going to a hotel for a threesome, and later on, a two-some with me. I think Mick wrote this about a famous singer with whom he "trysted," in a one-off sexual encounter. Though the pairing didn't last, the singer still thinks of her. I found each of these guys fascinating, more as transitory experiences than serious partnerships.

Like "Some Girls," the subject of a Rolling Stones song, "some men" stay on my mind, in particular - three men from my years with a country-western dance club. Oh – and another one I met online during my first ventures in cyberspace. I dated these men with hopes for something serious, but alas, none panned out. We had good conversations in all cases, dancing, in most cases, and concerts, in some cases.

I met Gil in a group for divorced and separated people where he recruited a few of us to come to the country-western dances for single people. Anyone could come, newcomers and experienced old-timers alike, to take lessons and find partners for both group and couple-type dancing. There we could blend our talk mode from the divorced group with physical activity and listen to music while meeting people too. He had met a woman, Susan, who became his partner for a number of years. He wanted the company of more like-minded people to join him at the dances and classes.

Good looking and great dancers and singers, Gil and Roland ruled the local country dancing singles club. From the start, Gil admired long-time club member Roland for his dancing skills, and I assume, his success with various women, me among them. Roland had learned to dance as a child back in his home country of Germany and had become a professional "caller" of the moves in tunes danced by couples in between the group dancing. Roland's dancing was so smooth, he made all of his partners look good. I compared Roland and another male dancer to Fred Astaire and Gene Kelly. Roland said he'd rather be Gene Kelly, relating to Kelly's athleticism and perceived masculinity. Once, before a dance, while setting up folding chairs for seating, tables for the ticket takers, and the music system, he and I sang most of the lyrics to "You Made Me Love You (I didn't want to do it.)" That was true for me, because he seduced me with his dancing and words: "You know, you're the most attractive woman here." I said, "Oh, really?" He knew I had gone out with another dancer, a younger guy, Michael, a few times, and apparently thought I was ready to switch to him.

He had recently come out of a long-time relationship with another dancer and was playing the field. At least three of us vied for his attention, before a fourth woman, Joanne, snagged him for a committed relationship. More than once, each woman would stake out a spot in a corner of the dance floor to ponder, "Who is Roland going out with after the dance, and possibly home with tonight?" In a tune played regularly, Shania Twain's voice advised, "Dance with the one that brought you," but Roland often arrived alone, heeding his own inclinations toward the end of the evening. I asked him if all the female interest was good for his ego. Ah, duh. He just looked at me, until I repeated the question. Then he said, "Yes."

Memorably when I returned from a trip, Roland slotted in an unexpected pick-up, offering me a ride home. We shared a few reunion kisses at the airport, and then went out to eat. It was Good Friday and he had a day off work: a very good Friday for me, happy as I was, for any time he was willing to offer to spend alone with me. On the nights he didn't choose me, I would often cry, but I accepted the situation. I wonder now if all that frequent changing of partners within each round of the circle dances encouraged my complacency. Then I think of how safe, secure, and happy I later felt dancing with Dean, whom I first met outside of the singles dance club, in the group for divorced and separated people where I had first encountered Gil. Despite our different spiritual/religious orientations and politics, Dean and I saw each other exclusively for about a year. While together, we traveled to and from each venue and shared virtually every dance each evening,

Of all of Roland's paramours, I was most leery of Joanne, because we competed directly for Roland's attention, and she played hard, to win. I left a regional dance conference to go stay with my friend Rob for the night, avoiding her after she wouldn't leave us alone, even though we rode there in Roland's car and he and I were supposedly staying together. On my return the next day, as we drove back to his house, Roland apologized for my rival's interruption of our interaction. She continued to call for much of the night, as she habitually did when I stayed with Roland, and even stopped by, banging on his door. I feared more drama would ensue, but Roland said, "Don't worry, just ignore her."

Once Joanne visited my house, uninvited. I knew she was coming, alerted by her phone messages. I turned off all of the lights, and sat very still, in the dark, with my black and white cat George on my lap, until the doorbell rang, pushed hard, twice in a row. George leapt straight up a couple of feet, and came down hard on my forearm, giving me the biggest scratch of my life. Joanne left a letter that I didn't open for months, warning me against staying with Roland. Finally, when taking me to the airport for a solo European trip, Roland told me Joanne had insisted on an exclusive relationship. You tell me now?

A short time earlier when the three of us met at his house, ostensibly to become friends, I heard the two of them speaking and then arguing loudly in German, Roland's native tongue. I knew then, it was no contest. When I came back, he offered me a place in his life if I would be his secret lover. No, thank you. Roland even told me, and Joanne confirmed, that her children appeared on the Jerry Springer show to complain about her on an episode featuring children of bad mothers.

Roland always said he thought I preferred Gil to him as my perfect man. I had to turn that over a few times in my mind. Gil, on the other hand, seemed to like that I was spending time with Roland. Once the four of us, Gil and Susan, his female companion, and Roland and I went out to dinner after a dance. Roland and I weren't that hungry, with me explaining, "We like to eat at home," meaning Roland's cooking. Roland nodded, as we squeezed the edges of our bodies together on our side of the booth, sitting as close as we could, snuggling.

If Roland and I were exclusive, we may have lasted much longer. Roland loved to sing and dance, and even appreciated the Rolling Stones. He seemed comfortable in his "front man" role, teaching "round dance," those slow-dancing classes, and relished being in the center of a crowd's attention, all eyes on him, as he whirled around the floor. Roland was Mick Jagger, the German-born version, incredibly sexy and charismatic. Mick has often compared dancing to sex. I saw his public flirting decrease when he promised another dancer to be faithful, sexually, and only dancing with her. I hadn't learned to completely reject men who simultaneously dated other women. The square dance scene came before meeting Danny the Dog, the worst case of that, after Roland.

I had worried that Roland might have assimilated an anti-Semitic heritage, growing up in Germany toward the end of WWII, and had waited for the issue to arise. One day he made an extremely anti-Jewish comment, after I told him no, I wasn't Catholic, as he thought, but brought up in the Jewish tradition, though without religious rituals or temple attendance. Much later a Jewish friend came up with a comeback. He said I could have told Roland, "Yes, Roland, you can tell all your Nazi-sympathizing friends and family members that you have slept with a Jewish girl." I learned years later from my cousin that I was one-quarter German, and though none of my ancestors had lived in Germany for generations, maybe I felt some ancient DNA connection.

A dance caller named Ernie liked to put unusual phrases into his routines. One night he sang out this line to direct the dancers: "All Christians go into the middle." Everyone except Roland, Gil, and I went in, out of protest against the discrimination the statement implied, and a statement of our non-religious orientations.

The ideal man "on paper," Gil represented every mom's dream for her daughter. Blond with rough-hewn, handsome features, a mesomorph, fairly tall, super-articulate, a good sense of humor—I can hear his ready guffaw now—he loved to dance with the country-western dancers, and in clubs to live bands or jukeboxes. His slow-dance style was always more freelance than conventional, dancing a kind of combination of foxtrot and waltz, depending on the time signature. You never knew where he would move his feet. He expected his partners to follow his lead, off the dance floor as well as on. He had stopped driving years before, leaving me to take us to clubs about twice a week, once we started going out after he and Susan had broken up. Gil always paid for gas, more than enough to cover the expense.

He rarely got enough sleep and if his deprivation reached high levels, he might cancel a date unexpectedly. He had a habit of disappearing, as I should have learned from observing him with Susan, who would often ask others, "Has anyone seen Gil?" Either from boredom with what was going on, or to make a call, after cell phones became popular, or just to spend some time in a rest room, Gil would leave the table, the dance floor, or wherever we were, without saying anything. If I objected to being left alone for a half hour or more, he would become irate, self-defensive, blaming me for getting upset.

Gil had sworn off sex after his wife dumped him for another man a few years before, and doubled down, when his last paramour who he intended to stay casual with, turned serious and demanding. During his first go-round with Susan, he heard some of my family was in town. He brought Susan to a downtown restaurant to have lunch with us. When he met my brother and his children, the kids, my niece and nephew, called him Uncle Gil, impressed by both his gentlemanly manners and his treating all of us to lunch, including me and Susan. Susan wanted sexual intimacy with Gil, and even bought a larger house with an extra bedroom and bathroom so Gil could have his own suite. Gil insisted he never intended to move in.

With me, Gil would engage in make-out sessions, sometimes intense, resulting in near-prone positions on couches in clubs. When kissing standing up, leaning into each other while balanced on our respective bar stools, other patrons would chide us to "get a room." He told me he wouldn't or couldn't have sex for two reasons: first, he didn't want to become emotionally involved, and second, he wasn't even sure his body could perform. After a few months of this, I asked if maybe he wanted to try Viagra, procured from my little bro, who sent me a little blue pill in the mail. Gil seemed terrified by the prospect, but after a few more months, he asked if maybe I was up for having sex with him. I said, no, half-kidding, "You couldn't handle it, Gil," parroting what he had explained to me before, when in fact, I was pretty sure by then that I had no business getting more physically attached to him through full-on sex. I knew I couldn't risk becoming more emotionally bonded, since he wouldn't want anything resembling a full-on relationship, with its commitments and obligations.

At a club where Buckwheat Zydeco played on a double bill with Tab Benoit, the crowd couldn't help moving to the beat. Gil went up front to observe, while I stayed near the back, talking to a couple of guys, catching as much of the conversation as I could over the music and crowd noise. Packed in, soon everyone danced and sweated to the reggae rhythms. Gil came to look for me, and found me in between the two men, dancing. They soon said they had to go and Gil got their numbers, trying to set up a threesome with me in a hotel with these two randy boys. Gil would rent the room and watch the three of us. After meeting Gil, and hearing he practiced celibacy, my brother had insisted Gil was gay. I didn't agree. He did have a kinky streak, though. I tried to lightheartedly brush off his threesome plan, but no, Gil was serious and kept trying to persuade me to go for the tryst. I took him home.

We split up after a year or so, when I said I couldn't go on as we were, after I drove him to meet his son outside of a government building near the courthouse and sat in my car for over an hour and a half, waiting. Gil didn't give details but I figured out that maybe his son had to defend himself before a judge, whether for a motor vehicle offense or something else. Additionally, he had allowed another woman, clearly interested in him, to pick him up and take him to our dance class. I missed him though, and shortly after, begged him to come back. Too late. He had already phoned Susan who took up where they had left off a year before. She demanded that he not accept any more rides from the other woman, a move I didn't have the courage to make.

Susan and I never discussed my going out with Gil, because he didn't want me to tell her. I protected both of them, afraid of his anger if I told her, after he forbade me to do so. He made securing that promise from me a condition of our going out together. She would not like that we kept that from her, and he would flip out if I revealed our dating to her. However, I strongly suspected she knew because mutual friends had seen Gil and me together at a play. He told them we just happened to run into each other, which seemed possible, since we both hung out in that neighborhood sometimes. Deciding to see a play last minute seemed less likely.

A new guy, Dean, came on the scene, a rare find: a nice-looking, courteous and quiet financial planner. Gil had recommended the group to him. Whenever he doubted if he liked the activity or the people, Dean liked to say, "What else are we supposed to do, sit on the couch and watch TV every night?" When I saw the older women crowded around him, I decided to see if I interested him at all. Yes, I did. We went to dances for almost a year before I asked him if he intended to kiss me at midnight on New Year's Eve. He said yes. We continued going out and then, one night, at his house, ended up having sex. It was satisfying to me, and to him, judging by the spaced-out smile spread across his face, his eyes closed in post-coital bliss. He took me home before he went to church with his adult children the next morning. That week at the dance class he showed me the sermon: his pastor had emphasized how unmarried people shouldn't be having sex. But he had been married before and raised three kids! No matter. Hmm, how would our relationship work?

Then outside of my house the next weekend, apparently having gotten over the sermon, Dean said he would very much like to repeat the sexual experience "as soon as possible." My house was a mess, as usual, and I didn't feel sure enough about where we were going to let him in. Soon he wrote that this other woman had noticed him and mentioned going to a dance. That was my "Dear Andee" letter. I said go ahead and the two went on to form a tight relationship, living together but not marrying. She was perfect for him, "a hard worker," as he said, impressed with her. She attended school, earning degrees while maintaining a full-time job. She cooked regularly and cleaned too, unlike me. Her politics and his were more in line than ours, and I think she belonged to a church. I heard that they went to a dance conference together but stayed in separate rooms. I couldn't have lived with that. I ran into him from time to time later on and we danced some, glad to see each other, and feeling the mutual chemistry. I could have tried much harder to keep Dean around, instead of giving up the only man from this dance world who was nice-looking, faithful and reliable, with a job, and an active sex drive.

Turning back to the online realm where I had met Danny, I found Julian, in an online discussion community. He demonstrated a facility with words, primarily expressed in his poetry, and later, on the phone, an appealingly posh English accent that really drew me to him. He came from a working-class section of the UK, changing his speech after his dad hit it rich and his parents sent him off to boarding school where the other boys mocked him for his origins. He and I had a vivid written correspondence, mainly through email. Our phone chats derailed when I discovered that his last ex-wife, the third of three, still spent time at his place, answering his phone, much to my shock. Triad, anyone? I had been entranced by Julian's humor, but had not paid enough attention to his difficult personality.

When we met in person in a city between our two residences, Julian knocked on the door of my hotel room, as I sat facing the door, sitting at my little table at the other end of the room, facing the entrance.

Me: Come on in, it's open.

Julian: (Opening the door.) Hi.

Me: Hi.

Julian: Andee, are you that happy to see me that you can't even stand up to greet me?

Stuck to the chair, I couldn't move. I hadn't expected Julian's pomposity, the arrogance of his in-the-flesh presentation. His head was thrown back, his legs apart, his arms stretched out, all his posturing emphasizing his short stature and thinning hair. We had both seen the other's pictures and were none too impressed, but this— this was more like real life. Hey, it actually was real life! O no, what am I going to do now? We had two days punctuated by conflicts such as him objecting to me asking our waiter to correct his placement of dishes when he served me Julian's food. At the same meal, Julian drew in his breath, horrified, when I reached over for one of his fries, after asking if I could try it, but not waiting long enough for an affirmative reply. Julian's lengthy rebuke replaced the assumed "yes."

We met another time after that; what was I thinking?

I forgot my purse on a walk to where he was scheduled to give a reading and we had to go back. He said, "Andee, you're purposely making me late." We were still almost an hour early, counting in the time lost retracing our path. Whew. No way would we get along. I later learned, too late, that his mom had tied him to the legs of the kitchen table to keep him corralled when he was younger. That could piss anyone off, for life. We stumbled along for a year or so without enough common interests or compatible qualities to overcome the obstacles of distance, past relationships, and jobs. I would have to leave a tenured position, and chance not obtaining another teaching job. Julian had already relocated countries and would never consider a big move again. Julian remarried for the fourth time after our split, to someone else he met online whose personality better matched his in feistiness. I assume she found him more physically, emotionally, and possibly, financially compelling, than I did.

Interlude: "Miss You": Name That Tune

I often played a Stones cassette in the car, and the one time I drove Roland back home the night before we split, I had the Some Girls album on with "Miss You" starting up. I turned it down out of respect for my passenger's taste, but Roland told me to crank it up. He said, "It's the Stones!" Meant to be heard loud, he implied. Okay, then.

Listening between sets of a band in one club, Gil would ask if it was the Rolling Stones on the jukebox. He couldn't recognize any of the slower songs. "Play With Fire," for example, would come on, and Gil would ask, "That's not the Stones, is it?" Yes, yes, it is. "Wild Horses" came on. "This one?" Uh-huh. Someone played "Just My Imagination." "Is that the Rolling Stones too?" Yes. The last time I waited for Gil to come back to the car, interminably, so it seemed, I played the soundtrack of Scorsese's Casino over more than once, a two-cassette set, four full sides with thirty-one songs, including the Chicago Symphony Orchestra's "Matthäus Passion." I bought it mainly for the film score version of the Stones' "Can't You Hear Me Knocking," which was left out of the official recording, unbeknownst to me when buying it. Devo's version of "Satisfaction" made it on there though, which was some solace.

Chapter 8
"You Can't Always Get What You Want": New Mexico and the Final Men

Sometimes, as the song goes, if "you can't (always) get what you want," "you get what you need". In my case, that was a modicum of so-so male companionship. Moving out of Ohio was a big deal. I had wanted to go west since Charlie's unemployment prompted us to consider a switch of regions. Before that, I dreamed of going to San Francisco, with the proverbial flowers in my hair, at least to visit, if not to live. Once in New Mexico, I met men of a wide range of ages, none working out long-term.

I want to tell you how I found my latest home. I went from the frigid, yet friendly, dairy state, Wisconsin, to the varied cities of northern and central Ohio, to at last, a more artistically and politically compatible southwest city in New Mexico. I changed states first to follow my then-husband Charlie, then to take my job teaching college, and ultimately to a place of my choice.

Toward the end of my full-time work life, I looked up the site that matched people with their best places to live, *Find Your Spot.com*, and plugged in my criteria. Leaving out areas that were too expensive, too large, and too cold, my answers landed me in two places in New Mexico. On advice to visit each in both the summer and the winter, I tried southern New Mexico first, Las Cruces. I met nice people, among them an artist and gallery owner who recommended the bed and breakfast owned by a companionable woman where I stayed when I came to town. A real estate agent tried to find a suitable dwelling to rent or buy within walking distance of Mesilla, where the quaint shops and coffee bar that I liked were. No luck. I could have lived with the climate, a very mild winter and hot summer.

Then an acquaintance introduced me to a friend who had moved to Santa Fe for a job. I had ruled out that city due to high housing costs. The Santa Fe guy asked if I had considered renting which is what he did. Renting? The last time I rented was, hmmm, hard to recall, maybe a quarter of a century ago. I briefly considered Taos, north of Santa Fe, where I went for a few writing workshops, but decided it was too small and remote for me. Then I signed on for a month in a vacation rental in March 2015 to see if Santa Fe was for me. Sure enough, it was love at first "live." The month turned into six weeks while I located a small but two-bedroom casita in a three-unit complex right near one of the gallery areas and within walking distance of the coffee house I liked. I hit it off with the landlord by wearing my cap with a tongue motif, beating out the two other people waiting behind me to see the property. She was a big Rolling Stones fan. I secured the property, went home, sold my house for about the same as I paid twenty years before and moved to Santa Fe three months later, leaving behind a few friends. I had finally escaped the Midwest!

When I visited Las Cruces, twice in February and once in the summer, for a month each time, I met Roy, whose wife had recently died. A year later, he thought he was ready for a relationship, and to some extent, I took him at his word. Younger by several years, he didn't question my age, never asking. We were completely wrong for each other. He brought out his guns and laid them on the kitchen table, just to shock me. The town had scheduled a rally against domestic violence at a shooting range, of all places. I asked Roy if he would go to it, figuring he would fit into the environment, if not the event, to let me know how it turned out. He never answered my request. On the good side, Roy was an excellent kisser, and he had a pleasing touch I noticed the one time I let his hands reach under my outer clothing, mainly around the waist area. His daughter told him she thought I was getting serious about him well before he could handle a committed relationship. Likely true. We split up, such that our relationship was. A year later he had met another woman, a more conservative person who seemed right for him. She may not have objected to his cigarette smoking, as I did, mentioning it to him once. He told me he'd only smoke when out of my presence and he kept to that promise. The smell of the smoke hung around him, off-putting and yet appealing, making me briefly reconsider ending my twenty-plus year abstinence from nicotine.

In Santa Fe, I met Carl in a coffee house, and we hit it off because, he said, I seemed like I was "easy to talk to." We also had a common interest in critical teaching and learning, and he asked me to review his upcoming book on the topic when the publishers readied it to send out. We talked a lot about race and ethnicity, his Hispanic family coming from the Bisbee, Arizona area. He wasn't planning on staying in Santa Fe, just working temporarily at a hotel, until he could land a full-time academic job. We agreed to meet at a movie, Jordan Peele's *Get Out*. He loved it, but it was a little too scary, too horror-oriented for me. I did like the caricatures of the white family members. Soon after, we met in the coffee house again and I mentioned I was retired. "What?" he asked, suddenly noticing my advanced age, or realizing what he hadn't before, that I was some years older than he was, maybe fifteen, I think, or even a few more. That was it. He even unfriended me on Facebook. So much for younger men, very much younger men, anyway.

I currently have an interesting and unavailable male friend who likes to say if we had met three years ago our relationship would be much different. We met at a museum training class for volunteer guides. He is older than me, some nine years, Graeme, from Australia, the first older man I've become close to since Charlie. I like his accent, his lanky looks and his full head of straight gray hair. More than the superficial, I enjoy his interest in contemporary art and Native American culture and artifacts. But, like Danny, he has a partner, and in this case, lives with her. We usually only see each other one day a week for a few hours, for coffee and then lunch. We talk about subjects ranging from habits of different cultures to personal annoyances of people around us, ones we know or just encounter. He is a curious fellow, an apt companion for my inquisitive temperament. We discuss how we want to stay lively and engaged in the world no matter our age.

He hasn't mentioned our friendship or meetings to his live in partner. He chose to tell me about her during our second meeting, explaining why he hadn't looked for me in the coffee house as he said he might. I told him recently that if I did find a boyfriend or serious partner I didn't know if I'd keep seeing him. We both really enjoy the other's company. Once in a while we go to a movie, usually involving art or artists such as a biography of Picasso's early days, and a recent animated film about a therapist who persuades his patients to steal famous paintings whose characters torment him in his dreams. No one else I know saw the film, *Ruben Brandt,*

Collector, playing for only a week at an art theater in town. To me, this movie represents the essence of our connection, a particular interest in offbeat, though beautiful works of art, with intellectual content.

What happens next for me, relationship-wise, I have mainly left to chance, although my gut tells me meeting in person first bodes better for a future than meeting online. That means I have to put myself out to join groups or attend functions, rather than sitting at home with my media. The last time I met someone on an online dating site, I ended up running from the scene. He looked nice enough, but the first red flag was the two books he laid on our table, volumes written by him and his ex-wife, with a photo of her face and upper body, apparently topless, on the cover of one. A glimmer that he might not see the books again once handing them over, had occurred to him, so he said, as if he had gone through this process before, when he offered to "lend/give" me these tomes. I had not asked for them, let me be clear, nor did I want to read them after glancing through them. After he ranted for some time about being sent to a special island for dissidents while serving in Vietnam, and still fearing enforcement of Army rules set down then, I was ready to leave. Then he added a story about his recalcitrant addict son living with him who refused to move out when he asked him to leave, and I got up to bolt. Luckily, I had cash and he had to go in to pay for his tea, not ordering anything to eat, another red flag, since we supposedly met for breakfast, I ran down the street, not wanting him to follow me to where I lived close by. He soon came out and chased me, calling out, while I ducked into a gallery doorway, hiding there, until he passed by.

I didn't hear from him, and, as I breathed more easily, about a week later, boom, a message from him appeared in the inbox of the dating site. It said, "When are we going to get together again?" I told him I wasn't interested, and added that, by the way, he couldn't get my name right, preferring "Annie," even after I corrected him a few times. He seemed startled by my negative answer, asking, "What about the books?" I had taken the books with me, not really considering leaving them on the table where he had pushed them in front of me. This action was left-over from my extreme people-pleasing attitude from the past, afraid to be myself for fear of a hostile reaction in words, or even violence behavior. I saw his offer at first, a simple gesture toward our commonality as writers. I had wordlessly accepted them before I had the chance to look at them closely, and to hear more about their contents and about him in our ensuing forty-five minutes of interaction. I said, "What about 'lend/give?'" That didn't fire up any synapses of remembrances for him. Feeling sorry for him about the books, I left them where we met with a note to the staff that a man would probably come in to retrieve them in the next day or two, or if not, feel free to give them away or toss them.

Chapter 9

"I'm Free":
Straight Female Desires Male Stones Fan

These days, "I'm Free... to do what I want," within financial and emotional limits, as long as I can keep my cat. Here, in my last chapter, or as Jane Fonda calls it, the "last act," I am relatively happy, content with my life. As far as men: well, who knows? I might come across someone like my male roommate and concert companion for recent Stones shows, "the nicest person in the world," a phrase I reserve for those kind, gracious people who come along once in a while. On the other hand, I may not; it's all about staying "free" from my patterns of going for unavailable or not-so-nice men.

The AA "Big Book" tells readers how to prepare a "lead," a three-part oral presentation of their journey from alcoholism to sobriety. In remembering and describing the men in my life, I've used these stages for guidelines to think about my relationships with men: where I was (or what I "used to be like"), what happened, and where I am now (or what I "am like now"). (*Alcoholics Anonymous,* 4th edition, 2001, p. 58).

135

The ups and downs of the major relationships in each of the previous chapters reflect the theme of "the triad" that runs from my family background, first with my parents, Jack and Betty, and then as the oldest of my three siblings. The triad, a three-person group, was first described by the sociologist Georg Simmel in the early 20th century. He observed that when all parties were equal, the triad could exist well, three people forming a stable, balanced group. If not, the triad often degraded into two people against one. Added to the basic inequality of parents and a child, my parents literally put me between them, asking me, no, forcing me, to take sides when they disagreed, leaving me torn and confused. My dad usually won. They prepared me for conflict in the outside world; I had learned not to let fear prevent me from engaging in it. I still had no clue about how to resolve it. I grew up observing the male parent raging out of control, with the female parent giving in, ultimately stuffing her feelings, neither mode particularly useful in conflict negotiation.

Since it felt like "home" to me, I kept choosing relationships filled with conflict, creating or joining in partnerships with issues I did not have skills to resolve. I knew from teaching the work of a husband-wife team of sociologists (Cuber and Harroff, *Five Types of Marriage*, 1971) that for "conflict-habituated relationships," both people need to argue to maintain the relationship. If one dropped out, refusing the fight, tired of the anger and resentment, the relationship would change form, or most likely dissolve. A constant excitement was a relatively positive outcome of the regular tension that arose from two people at odds, continuously expressing opposing views. I think my relationships with Arthur and Bobby, both alcoholics, most exemplified this pattern.

When I left home to join my fate with Charlie's, my family turned into a more typical family unit, two parents with two children close in age, a boy and a girl. I called them "the kids." My younger sister and brother had come along seven and ten years after me. We competed for favor with our parents, forming another early triad in my life, often devolving into two against one. After high school, they both went away to college and never came back. No wait, my sister returned for a few months before going out west for good. I stayed away for four years when I first got married, enjoying my life without my dad's wrath.

My mom wanted a girl-child more like herself: petite and neat, and practical. I suffered my father's overt verbal abuse over my weight, calling me "fat pig," while my mother bore her disappointment over my looks more subtly, buying me clothes to make me look slimmer. In my late teen years, Betty brought home a woman - only slightly older than me. Blonde, pretty and thin, Kitty wore glasses like me. By the way she introduced her, Betty demonstrated that she would have preferred Kitty for a daughter and that she might just adopt her. Ouch. Gee, mom, I wish I could have been different for you. My weight fluctuated through the years, from higher to lower and back again, to somewhat consistent in my later years. I believe that, along with the physical and verbal abuse, contributed to my lack of self-esteem, and my thinking I didn't deserve a partner who treated me well.

Growing up I had shaky self-esteem cracked through with criticism, both spoken and unsaid. My mom wanted me to be like her, and my dad, like him. Since they were not much alike, that caused confusion. Today the best label for each of my parents might be "narcissist," and yet they were products of their times. World War II produced unmentioned PTSD in my father, I'm sure. The mild-mannered Christian square dancer Dean told me his father had the same rage-a-holic patterns my dad Jack did after his war service. Betty fits the classic co-dependent, with her excuses and attempts to keep the peace. Not a country music fan, she nonetheless stuck to Tammy Wynette's lyrics in "Stand By Your Man": "But if you love him, you'll forgive him…Cause after all he's just a man." Betty wasn't the most affectionate parent; she was prone to air-kissing, maintaining her picture-perfect red lipstick. I had to put my arms out, murmuring, "C'mere, Mom," to get a hug.

Triadic situations recurred often in my relationships. I seemed to escape a triad with Charlie, although his work loomed large, almost as if it was a third party. Interestingly, at one point, after he had stopped working, I thought I might have turned into the "workaholic" we both called him, as I threw myself into my studies, research and teaching. With Sam, both of us were married, and put the other into the third-party role in a triad, by definition of lesser import than our spouses, at first, anyway, until both couples split up. Arthur had his first love, alcohol, his attachment to his artwork, and a couple of women hanging around the periphery, but I had no overt feminine rival. With Bobby, his connection to his mother was particularly strong. I finally realized she actively sabotaged his relationship with me, a problem for which she apologized, unexpectedly, after our ultimate break-up. Finally, Danny's primary partner didn't know about me, though she had found out about some of his other liaisons over time. With the miscellaneous men, there was Roland, Joanne and I, and then Gil, Susan and I, both triadic groupings, classic "love triangles," with one party at the top, the male puppet-master, pulling the strings, manipulating the other two.

In short, all of "my men" were unavailable, physically or emotionally or both, sometimes through their use (abuse) of alcohol, past or present. I felt at home with these types of relationships, considering how I grew up. More and more, these days, I need to face that both my parents abandoned me, not physically, but emotionally. Addiction runs through my life, not just other people's, but my own, my heavy cigarette-smoking for thirty years, my compulsive attachment to relationships and the feelings of drama and excitement, and since the 1990s, my fan love of Mick Jagger and The Rolling Stones. I go to the shows when I can, whatever the monetary cost, getting my "fix" of the magical Jagger energy and if possible, his attention.

Charlie, had feelings, of course, but stuffed his most negative emotions about me, he told me later, into that imaginary trap door in his mind, not accessing them until after we split up. He never told me about them during the marriage. In avoiding a mate like my father, I went for someone more like my mom, while I carried out my father's rage in my behaviors. Distancing ourselves from our marriage partners, Sam and I first bonded through our studies, and then became close or pseudo-close by smoking tons of marijuana (and cigarettes), no doubt fogging up our perceptions. Never did we see each other as permanent partners: just distractions, students having fun. Arthur showed me what living with an active alcoholic was like. His intelligence and creativity couldn't compensate for his mood swings and blaming of me for our issues, Arthur exhibited a righteous self-defense similar to my father's, as well as sharing Jack's creative talents with him. Bobby had stopped drinking through treatment and AA without addressing his emotional deficiencies, his immature manner of hiding behind mothers and girlfriends, letting those around make excuses for him, thinking all the while, "Oh, isn't he cute?" A recovering alcoholic and daily marijuana user, with a girlfriend, Danny was a no-go from the start.

Sometimes, okay, often, the line between love and lust blurs for me, and, often, not in a good sense. Sex and love—I would get those mixed up, both in my attraction and the man's attraction to me. Actually, I usually knew the person wasn't good for me, but I would fall in love, from a little to a lot, if I had sex with the guy. Even when I know the physical urge didn't translate to emotional closeness, I pursued it. Only hurt results from that—well, pain with some kicks, or adventures, one might say. The connectedness I sought from love, I found I could manufacture from sexual contact, temporarily, anyway. But eventually, the warmth and simpatico feelings circling the lust would disappear, on my side, as well as the man's, leaving me empty, the physical desire draining away too.

For a time, I thought I knew something from studying marriage and the family that I could to apply to relationships in the real world. Then I came to a solid wall, like the final house built by the last of the three little pigs: a wall made out of brick, first with Charlie and then with Arthur. Without someone to co-create functional dynamics, one person alone cannot easily change a relationship. Without someone to acknowledge that the patterns are screwed up, one person cannot do much to fix it. Also, hey, I admit my own blind spots and lack of role models growing up did contribute to the problem. How do people do it, calmly talk together to figure out and negotiate each other's preferences, without triggering inappropriate anger or fear? In my family we had to get so upset, in a rage or crying in frustration or grief, to even begin to address interpersonal problems.

I learned to wait a while, at least until the third date or three weeks, or more, to sleep with someone. I learned that some of the pitfalls were my fault, not the men's, such as not setting boundaries on what I wanted and needed, the way Susan did from Gil, for example. You have to have self-esteem, confidence, and a willingness to lose someone to do that, and also - tire of the pain that outweighs the ephemeral feelings of belonging, of closeness. Another "aha "moment for me came when I read an article about relationships that said each argument is not about ending the relationship, but can work toward resolving an issue, without a life-and-death tone. This communication skill might have helped me with Arthur, Bobby, and Gil.

I had to teach myself over the years to set limits on others' expectations, to say no to requests too difficult or unreasonable, according to ME. I have worked on anger issues, and not taking slights too personally. I've made progress, am calmer than I was, helped by twelve-step meetings and advice I've sought from friends.

Animals have helped satisfy my desires for companionship and affection. I never had a dog of my own, but I love them. Well, maybe knowing Danny came closest to that, animalistic as he was, usually accompanied by his own dear pup. He certainly reignited my sexuality, reframing it as a powerful, crucial life force.

Most of the time since my marriage, I have lived alone, except for Arthur and on and off with Bobby and brief sojourns with Danny. I've had cats, a sister and brother pair for almost fourteen years, went five years without a pet, and now have a white Siamese-domestic mix, "Sunny," super-intelligent, ornery and very affectionate. She cuddles under the covers in bed, especially during the colder months.

An evolutionary path for me has been learning to be alone. From the stories of young women I talk to today, Uber drivers or children of friends, I gather that most of the women of this next generation learn they don't need partners to survive, economically or even emotionally, the key factor. Not until my job was in jeopardy during my relationship with Bobby did I finally reach the point of accepting my solitary condition. I had to break the tie with Bobby to keep my job and stay sane.

What about the good ones who got away? Jake from college, the first time around, who took care of me when I barely had change for the ramen noodles. He comforted me. I called him decades later, and sure enough, still married to his first and only wife, he sounded just a nice as ever. A dark blonde, he had handsome chiseled features, and was very short in stature, like me. Or that dark-haired, really sweet man from one of my psychic seminars who the leader advised me to turn to after he saw me flirting with a bad boy in his class. My friend from grad school and I recently reviewed our choices in men, concluding that we did find bad boys attractive, short of those with criminal records. We both found them exciting, not as boring as the good boys.

Trouble is, bad boys are just Not. That. Nice.

So how did this innocent bookworm from Milwaukee turned rock 'n roller keep her basically upbeat, cheery and even hopeful attitude toward life, men and relationships? My childhood readings contributed greatly. Like Pippi Longstocking, I had faith I could rise above less than fortunate circumstances, including destructive relationships. Pippi's mother had died shortly after Pippi's birth. After her father fell overboard off his ship, not to reappear, as she departed for dry land, Pippi told the other sailors "Don't worry about me. I'll always come out on top" (Lindgren, 1950).

Pippi's unconventional appearance always appealed to me too, from top to bottom: two red braids that stood straight out from her head, a homemade blue dress patched with red, two different colored stockings, with much-too-big shoes, bought by her father to allow room to grow. Like Mick Jagger, she seemed her own person, impervious to criticism of hairstyle or clothing. I never liked the curly hair of my early life, and worked hard to straighten it, to "straighten it out" to fit in. Pippi and Mick helped me not only to survive my difference from most others, but to celebrate my uniqueness later on. I learned to value my understandings of minority groups and outcasts of all sorts, and my acting, speaking, and writing abilities, such as they are.

Another noted nonconformist, Lawrence Ferlinghetti chooses to go with the "yea-sayers" instead of the "nay-sayers," he says in *The New York Review of Books* (September 26, 2019, p. 37.) Turning 100 years old in 2019, Ferlinghetti still co-owns the Bay area bookstore *City Lights* that he and his friend Peter Dean Martin started in 1953. His rocky childhood, spent mainly with his aunt and other surrogate parents did not make him bitter, but rather spurred his creativity and the retention of a youthful, playful, if rebellious spirit. Exposed to American and European literature of the 19th and 20th centuries, he says he valued much of it, but picked the positive writers over the negative, such as T. S. Elliot, known for *The Wasteland*. He sides not with the "Poets of Loss," but with the "yes-sayers," such as Walt Whitman and Henry Miller. Me too.

When Charlie and I saw Ibsen's *A Doll's House* he could envision us as the characters, him as the dry, bossy, master of the house Torvald, and me as Torvald's younger, obedient, yet dissatisfied and then rebellious, wife Nora. When Nora slammed the door, leaving Torvald and their children, just before the curtain closes, Charlie turned to me and said, "That's you." I told him that if so, he would have to be Torvald. He stayed silent, nodding in assent. I replied, "I don't think you're that bad." Well, I did leave him, but with no children, intentionally declining the opportunity to have them with him. No regrets on those scores. I'm free. I've read *A Doll's House Part 2*, written recently, to see what happened in another author's mind to Nora and Torvald.

In this modern sequel by Lucas Hnath (2017), Torvald asks Nora if, with her partners since him, she ever achieved what she desired before she left him: "I'm talking about two people spending time together, figuring out how to be around each other." She says no and asks him the same question, if he has ever found that. He says no also. I'm not sure if a "rest of your life" person is possible for me. But at least I escaped from the doll's house. I don't want to lie to someone and not be who I am for the sake of a relationship, as Nora in Part 2 declares.

My experience is, of course, not as illustrious as Jane Fonda's, either in my own achievements, or in my relationships. Hers are depicted in her 2018 documentary for HBO, *Jane Fonda in Five Acts*. My men don't compare to her father and her famous husbands in her first four acts: Henry Fonda, actor, Roger Vadim, director, Tom Hayden, activist, and Ted Turner, media mogul. But I did cycle through men with diverse careers, from a computer programmer, Charlie, to a sociologist, Sam, to an artist, Arthur, to an audio/visual technician, Bobby, and lastly, to a musician, Danny.

I hope the final chapters of my life at least somewhat mirror her last act, which is a paean to the independent woman, herself/myself, and a growing number of women everywhere, whether alone or in intimate relationships.

To live now where I've chosen, independent of full-time job or man, I notice many of us residents of "the city different," Santa Fe, feel grateful we are here, even in the wintertime, without hurricanes or earthquakes. At times that winter resembles the Midwest, never for very long though. Without a partner, relatives nearby or a mortgage, I am truly free to leave or go as I wish, not counting moving expenses. But I feel like staying put. I feel at home.

The Final Interlude: "It's Only Rock 'n Roll": My History with the Band

Some of my own history with the Rolling Stones is described in my 2014 book You Get What You Need *(Miniver Press, 2014) where fans describe how they became Stones "fanatics." I interviewed over one hundred people from various countries who were members of online fan clubs. Ever since my parents expressed shock upon seeing the boys on Ed Sullivan in 1967, I have followed their careers and their musical output. I didn't hear them in person until the "Voodoo Lounge" tour of 1994, upping my attendance over time from local shows to two across the pond to London in 2007 and then further to a show in Amsterdam in 2017.*

This year, 2019, I will likely see Mick Jagger at concerts postponed from his heart valve surgery, including his first appearances with the band at Soldier Field in Chicago, in Denver, and in Miami, bringing my good friend I met in grad school in the '70s to her very first show. May the Stones and their fans rock on indefinitely!

As for my own future, I quote what Mick said in Las Vegas between songs the day he flew back to the States from visiting his hospitalized father in London. After taking the call finding out his dad had died shortly before he went onstage, he said softly into the microphone, looking down: "You never know."

Epilogue:
"(This Could Be) The Last Time": Seeing Mick

Sweaty and slightly bruised from the woman's attack on me—her way of objecting to letting another person near what she saw as "her" prized spot—I finally had another "encounter" with Mick Jagger in 2019, while in the company of some 50,000 people in Soldier Field in Chicago. Not wanting any more people sharing the front row rail partway down the catwalk, in Pit 2, on Keith's side, the woman physically protested with jutting and jabbing elbows and knees. Before I slid in next to her, looking to her right and left, I saw plenty of space on either side of her. She had already succeeded in causing a tall man discomfort, his whole body scrunched inward from her efforts to eject him from the spot, saying, as the man on his other side and I extricated him, "I can't watch the show like this." I took his place between her and a husband and wife team I had spent the last several hours with, waiting in line until security moved all of us, the whole crowd, because of rain, costing us our vastly better places near the front of the line. I had begun to try to reason with the woman, to stop her jamming her limbs into me, speaking softly to her, telling her "I'm

149

sure we can work this out," when, in an innocent voice, she called out, "Security!" The security guy, having observed her behavior, told us, "I think you can work this out yourselves." Whew.

Not too long after that, she yelled out, "Yeah, Andee!" What? In a stadium filled with fans, she recognized me. Six years ago, we had bought tickets together, strangers, but part of an online fan group, and got really lucky with our Lucky Dip lottery tickets, landing in the small tongue-shaped pit for a Philly arena show. As I felt her elbows and knees pulling back some, I said, "You can't be mad at me now, can you?" Just then another fan stepped out of our row into the second row, because, she later told me "You both apologized." Wow. Plenty of room for all. The same fan patted me on the back after Mick stopped and looked into my eyes for a long pause in his routine. Yeah, Mick, that was me, you know, from that small crowd in New York? When you improvised "eight kids" in your song, I laughed. You caught my eye, and knew I got it, your latest number of children, the last one, a toddler, Dev, already dancing to your music, another Sagittarius, like Keith and me, fire signs, compatible with yours, Leo the Lion.

ABOUT THE AUTHOR

Andee Baker (Andrea J. Baker) taught sociology and conducted research in Ohio until her retirement as an Associate Professor in 2014. Her interests have centered round gender roles, deviance, and internet communities, relationships, and identities. She studied eighty couples who met online and then offline, producing early research on internet relationships, summarized in her book *Double Click: Romance Among Couples Who Met Online* (Hampton Press, 2005). With Monica Whitty and James Inman, she co-edited *Online Matchmaking* (Palgrave MacMillan, 2007), a collection of studies of aspects of online dating. Writing for popular audiences, Andee interviewed over one hundred members of online fan communities for *You Get What You Need: Stories of Fans of the Rolling Stones* (Miniver Press, 2014). They told her about their first exposure to the music, their concert experiences, their Stones memorabilia, and how they connected to like-minded fans, online and in person.

Since 2005, Andee lives in New Mexico with her white cat Sunny, and continues to follow The Rolling Stones as much as time and money allow. She likes to act in plays whenever possible, and occasionally writes essays about everyday life.